Copyright © 1961 by Margaret Burnaby

MADE AND PRINTED IN GREAT BRITAIN FOR
HODDER AND STOUGHTON LIMITED, LONDON
BY C. TINLING AND CO. LIMITED, LIVERPOOL,
LONDON AND PRESCOT

THINKING THROUGH THE CREED

Addresses in a College Chapel

by

HUGH BURNABY

Late Fellow and Dean of
Emmanuel College
Cambridge

*With an introductory Memoir
by E. Welbourne, Master of
Emmanuel College*

London
HODDER AND STOUGHTON

THINKING THROUGH
THE CREED

HUGH BURNABY
(1889–1956)

A Memoir by E. Welbourne,
Master of Emmanuel College, Cambridge

Hugh Burnaby was born on 15 November, 1889, at the Rectory of Etton in the East Riding of Yorkshire. His father, the Reverend John Charles Wellesley Burnaby, moved from Etton in 1894 to become vicar of St. Mary's, Beverley, and thence in 1898 to the Rectory of Asfordby, a Leicestershire village with which his family had been almost continuously connected since another Hugh Burnaby held the benefice in the middle of the seventeenth century. Most of our Hugh's boyhood was spent there. From Haileybury College he won a scholarship at Jesus College, Cambridge, and took a First Class in both Classical and Theological Triposes. After a year at Leeds Clergy School under R. H. Malden he was ordained in 1915 to the parish of Swinton in Lancashire as Curate of B. O. F. Heywood, afterwards Bishop. In 1918 he enlisted in the R.A.M.C., from which he transferred as a Private to the Coldstream Guards—though too late to see active service. On demobilisation he returned to Swinton, and was for a short time head of a hostel for ex-service candidates for Ordination studying in Manchester University. In 1921, at the age of thirty-one he was recalled to Cambridge as Fellow and Dean of Emmanuel in succession to C. E. Raven; and there he stayed for the rest of his life.

He was appointed to a University Lectureship in Divinity, and lectured chiefly on the New Testament, as well as undertaking the heavy work of teaching elementary Greek to men who at times found it difficult to believe that the Scriptures had not been revealed in seventeenth-century English. But he did not wish to confine his work to men seeking ordination, or to that minority of ordinands who read Theology. He was at the service of every member of the college who needed his help, or found pleasure and happiness in his friendship. He was President of the College Boat Club, and in a succession of bad years upheld it in its courage, spending hours on the towpath. He founded, and until the war maintained, a College Dramatic Society, giving it the wise advice that it was no insult to an audience to entertain it, and no great wisdom to allow a college play to make an end of the work men came to Cambridge to do. He himself was a superb actor, with a beautiful speaking voice, and a joy in kindly mimicry of the follies of mankind. But most he rejoiced in teaching young men to sing, men who often had no knowledge that this feat was possible for them. He showed how a singer could make his words heard and understood. The "Emmanuel Singers" met weekly in his rooms for coffee, catches, glees, and Gilbert and Sullivan, and made the end-of-term concert at times a noisy riot.

As an undergraduate he had been a man of legendary silence. His silence remained as an essential part of the man, in no way a cause of the discomfort which silence often creates. He helped others by listening, and men learned thus that they had come to Cambridge to learn. As by listening he encouraged others to speak of their beliefs, of their doubts, even of their disbeliefs, so he knew that from time to time he must face the duty of speaking. He had listened to others: they had a right to ask him what he had to say.

His sermons were delivered in the Chapel which Archbishop Sancroft caused Wren to build. There is no pulpit, and the preacher stood on the steps of the altar. Behind him hung a picture of the Return of the Prodigal Son. Whether, as some freshmen seem to be told before they enter it, the plain simplicity of the Chapel is a witness to the sound Protestant tradition of the college, whether its conscious beauty is a return to an older tradition of the Church which had survived Puritan oppression during the Civil War, whether indeed the Chapel was inspired by the new buildings in the countries recaptured by the Jesuits for Rome, is unknown. It is an easy building in which to preach, and Burnaby could make every word heard as plainly as if he had been speaking to half a dozen men in his rooms, or to a man alone. He was speaking among friends and to friends, and there was no show of the orator's art and indeed no need for its use.

The memory of the long years when Emmanuel was a parsons' college—as indeed were most of the colleges—still persists; but long before Burnaby came to Emmanuel, scientists in it outnumbered ordinands. Its Protestant tradition, often a misunderstanding by others of its religious duty, drew to it men brought up in the sincerity of dissenting homes, who thought with truth that their coming would not be unwelcome. It drew also a good many men of evangelical beliefs; but in Burnaby's later years he was likely to encounter the undergraduate from a home which had little memory of religion, where the parents were as troubled at the news of their son's baptism, as once were Victorian parents at his loss of belief.

During this latter part of his time, when the bulk of freshmen came into residence from national service, he was not preaching to schoolboys but to grown men with more experience of the world than many who have been protected from it by school and home and college, and even by the ministry of the Church into which they have gone. Burnaby tried to make it possible for any man to attend Chapel who found himself able to venture through its doors. He knew that side by side there would be sitting men whose traditions of worship and belief were very different, and perhaps altogether lacking. To him, the Prayer Book, the language of the Church of England, the language of the Catholic Church through the centuries of belief, was a known language. To many of them it was a new language, often one without meaning, at times one with a meaning debased by ignorance which had persuaded itself it was understanding. Maybe he was not a great scholar, but he was an educated man. He knew that educated men, to reach understanding and agreement, must use words consciously, carefully, and by discussion discover whether behind verbal difference lies agreement, whether behind apparent agreement lies undiscerned difference.

The series of talks on the Creed which this book contains, however, was addressed not to the Sunday congregation of some 150 men of very mixed background, by no means all Anglican in upbringing, and not always Christian, but to a smaller gathering on a weekday evening, chiefly if not wholly Anglican, and conscious of its religious attachment, and perhaps of the possibility of ordination. Such men, who had come together in a Cambridge college, were learning that the religion of their friends might well be neither in statement nor in worship the religion in which they themselves had been brought up; that the problem for them to face was the certainty of their friends which matched their own sincerity; that it could not be faced by assuming that there were no differences or that there ought to be no differences, or by the expectation that the other man must accept what they had no wish themselves to change. They were learning also what questions their friends asked, and what questions they found less easy of answer than the Church was believed to assume; that some meaning was expected, in those who spoke familiar words, by those to whom the words were unknown; and that difference might be of itself a way to understanding, ought not to be a way to break friendships, or to compel avoidance of knowledge even of the existence of difference.

In these as in all his Chapel sermons Burnaby was preaching to men who saw him daily, and, as the village knows its parson, knew him better out of Church than in it. He was conscious of his own belief, conscious also of the imperfection of his understanding, and of the difficulty of explanation. If his every sermon was to the text "Lord, I believe, help thou my unbelief", his daily life was to a different text: "Blessed are the meek."

He never married. His brother's children and the children of his friends made for him a family, and children adored him. In 1956 he was due to retire from his Lectureship in a year's time, and it was in his mind to move then to some parish where he could give as much help as might be possible to some over-worked friend—seeking, as was his habit, the lowest room. But he had already begun to suffer from heart trouble, and the last attack came as he returned to the Chapel vestry after celebrating on the morning of Wednesday, 9 May. He died within twenty-four hours, as Ascension Day was dawning.

THINKING THROUGH
THE CREED

Editorial Note

The addresses which are here printed were written
out before delivery, like all my brother's sermons,
in a very small hand with many abbreviations;
but it has been possible to reproduce them for the
present purpose in a form which called for very little
in the way of editing, beyond the insertion of refer-
ences for Scripture quotations. My brother was fond
of introducing phrases which had struck him in his
reading, without attaching to them the names of
their authors when these were unlikely to be familiar
to his hearers. Usually he was careful to indicate
his indebtedness by a label such as "someone has
said", or "it has been truly said". Sometimes, however, the only indication of borrowing is the use of
inverted commas in the manuscript; and in the
printed text this silent form of acknowledgement has
generally been preferred, in order to avoid tedious
repetition of the formulae of quotation.

J. B.

1

The Apostles' Creed

The subject for our thinking is to be the Apostles' Creed. And before we begin on the Creed itself, something should be said by way of introduction. The Apostles' Creed was not, of course, the work of the Apostles. An ancient tradition that, in solemn assembly, the twelve Apostles drew up a Creed, each Apostle making his own contribution, is no more than a pious fiction. Indeed, the Creed did not reach the exact form in which we know it until the eighth century. But, so far back as the second half of the second century, it is possible to trace the existence in the Church of Rome of a creed which, except for a few later additions, closely resembles our Creed. And following so closely, as it does, what may be called "credal themes" to be found in the New Testament, it may claim to represent "Apostolic" teaching. We may take it as a fair summary of what Origen (in the third century) called "the first elements of a simple faith", elements that were taught to candidates for baptism.

Now, we should notice at the outset the word "in" after "I believe". I believe *in* God—*in* Christ—*in* the Holy Spirit. The preposition *in* is of outstanding importance. To believe *in* someone, is to put your trust in him. The Christian faith is not, primarily, intellectual assent to certain doctrines, but trusting in

God, as Christ has revealed Him. The Christian
revelation did not take the form of a system of doctrine, but of a human life; and what we find in the
Creed is a statement of how the Church interpreted
the significance of that life. Such an interpretation
was essential. But its purpose was to sustain that faith
in God, which the life and death of Christ had gener-
ated; and the statements of the Creed can claim our
acceptance because they have been found, in centuries of Christian experience, to do that. Yet it
remains true that the essence of Christian faith is not
the acceptance of doctrinal statements but devotion
to Christ, and trust in Him as Saviour. Such trust
is possible for one who cannot fully understand all
the articles of the Creed, one who has not the intellectual capacity to think out all the implications
of his faith, or to examine the grounds on which it is
based. Such a person can say the Creed, even if he
does not understand all that it means. To accept the
Christian faith, it is not necessary to be an "intellectual". At the same time, we ought to use such
brains as we have, to examine "the Faith"—the
Church's interpretation of the fact of Christ—as it
is set forth in the Creed. That will be our object in
these chapters.

As we go through the various clauses of the Creed,
there are a few things which we shall need to bear
in mind.

(1) We must remember that the Apostles' Creed
was drawn up in an age in which men thought of the
world very differently from the men of today. *We*
do not think of heaven as a place above the sky, nor
of hell or Hades as a place under the earth. And so we,
if we were to try and draw up a new Creed, would not

speak of Christ as descending into hell, ascending into heaven and destined to come down again from heaven to earth to judge the living and the dead. But the faith which we confess in the Creed is not tied to a particular form of expression. Indeed, if we insist on taking all the Creed quite literally, we may well miss the spiritual truth which the men of another age than ours were trying to express. The Creed needs continual re-statement, as man's understanding of the world in which he lives grows and changes. Indeed, we may go further than this. There may even be some things in the Creed which, in their literal sense, we may feel unable to accept at all. That need not disturb us greatly. What matters is not the literal statement, but "the religious conviction, the spiritual reality, to which the literal statement points". And as we go through the Creed, that is what we shall continually be trying to discover.

(2) But, in that case, we may well feel inclined to say: "Would it not be better to draw up a new Creed, which would express the old truth in the thought-forms of the present day?" An obvious answer to that is that it would need the agreement of the whole Church of Christ—and in its divided state, such agreement could hardly be obtained. But, apart from that, I question whether it is really desirable. The Creed must continually be *re-interpreted*; but there is much to be said for keeping the old Creed, just because it *is* an old Creed. However differently we may express our faith, it is still essentially the same faith that we profess. And of that, the recitation of a Creed which has come down to us from the early days of Christianity is a pledge and reminder. It "brings down to our generation a weight of tradition

which we shall ignore at our peril". So it was that the Christians of long ago expressed their faith. That faith we share. That faith the Creed contains. And it is to that faith, and not to its literal expression, that we are committed when we say the Creed.

2

I believe in God

We might perhaps have expected the Christian Creed to begin with a confession of belief in Christ—the Revealer of God. But historically, of course, belief in God comes first. The mission of Jesus was not to unbelievers: the Old Testament, which His hearers knew, is still part of our Bible, and tells how God revealed Himself in the history of Israel before the coming of Christ. And therefore the Creed rightly begins with a declaration of belief in God, even though the full meaning of that belief depends upon belief in Christ, which comes afterwards. Now we have already seen the importance of the preposition "in". Belief *in* God means not merely belief that God exists, but trust in Him. Such trust can only follow upon personal knowledge of God: it is only one whom we *know* that we can really trust. To the fullness of such knowledge we may hope to attain, but the attainment is perhaps not given to everyone. There may be some who must depend for their belief on something less than personal knowledge of God. And therefore it is worth while to enquire what grounds there may be, apart from such knowledge, for believing that the world is in the hands of a transcendent power that is friendly, and that we can trust.

We must admit at once that we shall not find reasons that would satisfy the scientist—quâ scientist. The existence of God is not susceptible to that kind of proof. We must look elsewhere for the evidence that we seek. It has been said—I do not know with how much truth, but by one who did not use his words lightly—that "neither history nor geography can show us any tribe or people which is devoid of all religious awareness". Religion of some kind is a universal phenomenon. And we are bound to ask, "Why? What causes man's religious awareness? Why is he hungry not only for bodily food, but for the Bread of Heaven?" We can't dismiss it as wishful thinking. "If we have been given deceiving souls, how can we argue that we have been given trustworthy intellects?" Surely there can be but one explanation of the fact of man's spiritual hunger. That a godless world—a world in which the idea of God is an illusion—should somehow have produced in men a longing which it can never satisfy, is less easy to believe than that "God has made us for Himself", and that that is the reason why, as Augustine said, "our hearts are restless until they rest in Him". Is it likely that a restless soul after seeking rest everywhere else in everything that on an atheistic hypothesis is alone real, and failing to find it, should find it at last in that which has no basis in reality at all?

Such reasoning as this may well lead to the conviction that the existence of God is a necessary hypothesis even though the final proof, which can only come from personal knowledge of God, is lacking. Yet I often wonder whether those who disown such knowledge may not be deceiving themselves. "God speaks to us through ourselves." And he does not speak to everyone through the same medium. Yet it is His voice, if he did but know it, that artist, musician, philosopher, or scientist, hears. "Whatsoever things are lovely, whatsoever things are true, whatsoever things are honourable"—may not our love for these things, our devotion to them, our delight in them, be itself, did we but know it, love of God, the God who reveals Himself to us through these things? To follow the light that we can see is a way to knowledge of God. For it leads to the conviction that unless all we hold most dear is illusory, the universe must be in the hands of One who loves the things that we love, and can ensure their conservation.

Now, if all this is true, it follows that our idea of God must be determined by what we ourselves see to be the highest. We must think of Him as one who embodies our highest ideals. Of course, we cannot comprehend God completely: if we could, He would not be God. But we must at least believe that He is the highest we can conceive. It is often complained that man makes God in his own image. But if we are to form any idea of God at all, we must use human analogies; and that to do so is not wholly mistaken, is verified to some extent by the results to which it has led. As the Dean of St. Paul's has said: "The one progressive line of religious evolution is connected with the application to the divine of the analogy of human life and experience." Along this road "the believing mind has travelled from superstition to noble creeds". That is at least some reason for thinking that it is not the wrong road. For the Christian, at least, it is fundamental. Believing that in the human life of Christ is to be found the clearest revelation of the nature of God that has ever been made, or in the conditions of human life ever can be made, he has no alternative but to suppose that human nature cannot be altogether alien to the God who used it as the medium of His own self-revelation. "He that hath seen Me," said the Christ of St. John, "hath seen the Father" (John xiv: 9). If that is anthropomorphism, then to anthropomorphism the Church is irrevocably committed.

3

I believe in God the Father

So the Apostles' Creed begins. We have considered the justification for thus describing the nature of God in terms borrowed from human ideas and human activities. We must now begin to consider each of these attributes of God in turn. Firstly—the *Father-hood* of God. "After this manner therefore pray ye," said Jesus: "Our Father." And St. Paul bore witness to the depth of experience which that name for God expressed, when he wrote to the Christians in Rome: "Ye received the spirit of adoption, whereby we cry 'Abba, Father'" (Romans viii: 15). There are titles for God, it has been said, without which a religion would not be itself; and for Christianity the supreme title is that of Father.

But what meaning was the title intended to convey?
Not simply, as in other religions, that God is the
source of life, and that the world owes its existence to
Him. That idea is perhaps included in the word. But
its real purpose, I think, was (1) to express the specifically Christian conviction that the essential characteristic of God is *love*; and (2) to guard against mistaken
ideas of the *nature* of God's love. For "love" is a word
which has a very wide range of meaning. And to
speak of the love of God may be very misleading,
unless we have a clear idea of what is meant by it.
Now, it is significant that to express what they meant
by the love of God, the New Testament writers had
to find a new word. The ordinary Greek word for
"love" would not do, so they used a rare word,
agapé, for which we have no exact equivalent in
English. But we shall not go very far wrong if we say
that the love of God for man is like the love of a
father for his child. Such love is the nearest human
counterpart to the divine love. Let us follow this out
and see where it leads us.

(1) The love of God, like the love of the ideal
father, is a wholly *unselfish* love. We commonly love
other people, because in some way or other we find
them attractive—because they satisfy a desire or a
need of ours. Our love is to that extent selfish. *God*
loves us—and here a father's love for his child is
akin—for ourselves; and His love expresses itself in a
concern for *our* highest good. There is no comparison,
therefore, between His love, and that of the kind of
father who is so far indifferent to his children's good,
that, as we say, he "spoils" them. Such love—selfish
as it is—is wholly unlike the love of God. To suppose,
then, that God can ignore the evil which threatens

our true welfare, is to misunderstand the very nature of His love. It is the love of a *holy* God, who would have His children holy as He is holy. And it has been truly said that "it is only safe to approach the doctrine of the divine love through the doctrine of the divine holiness".

From this, then, it follows: (2) that the love of God is not necessarily incompatible with His permission of pain and suffering. C. S. Lewis remarks in one of his books that many of us seem to want not so much a father in heaven, as a grandfather—someone who only wants to see us enjoying ourselves. But experience seems to show that unalloyed enjoyment is not the best thing for us. "It is good for me," said the Psalmist, "that I have been in trouble" (Psalm cxix: 71). And I think most of us would agree that it is not the things that cost us the least effort that bring us the truest satisfaction. We thrive on difficulties and hardship. And the father who really loves his child does not try to shield him from the discipline that makes a man of him. Yet much of the suffering of the world appears to serve no such purpose of good, and to go far beyond what might seem to be required for the formation of character.

And that brings us to (3) a third aspect of the Fatherhood of God. An old member of this college, who was for many years a missionary in Burma, wrote there, shortly before the Japanese invasion, a little book called *God and Human Suffering*. It contains the following illustration of one aspect of God's Fatherhood: "A child wakes up in the night to find the house on fire: the terror and calamity are great enough—but they are relieved if the child finds his father coming through the flames and wreckage, intent on his rescue. The child may wonder how such calamity could be, or may be stunned by the pain and terror of it. But at least he is saved from the agony of the feeling that there is no one to help him, and that his parents do not care." That God *does* care is what Christ revealed in His death on the Cross. "With those who love Him," said St. Paul, "God co-operates in all things for good" (Romans viii: 28). And that is why, in the face of what might seem to belie his hopes and destroy his faith, the Christian can still trust his heavenly Father.

Such is the Christian belief in the Fatherhood of God. The grounds of that belief should become clearer as we go on. For the present it is enough to say that it is based not simply on the fact that *Jesus* believed and taught it—though that is something. The Christian belief about God has from the very beginning rested less on what Jesus taught, than on Jesus Himself—on the conviction that "God was in Christ", and that "he who had seen Christ had seen the Father".

4

I believe in God the Father Almighty

I believe, that is, in a God who is both all-loving and all-powerful. And we are confronted at once with the problem of reconciling that faith with the existence of evil in the world. The Dean of St. Paul's has described in one of his books how, as a boy, he was suddenly so overwhelmed by it that, for a moment, he lost all faith in God. "If God *can* prevent evil and does not, He is not benevolent; and if He *would* prevent evil, but cannot, He is not *Almighty*." That is the old dilemma. Is there any way by which it can be resolved?

Now it has been said with truth that "faith raises many of the mountains that it has to remove". And this particular mountain is a misunderstanding and misuse of the word "Almighty". We assume that "Almighty" must mean "able to do everything". But we need only reflect for a moment to see that such omnipotence cannot be ascribed to God. It is surely obvious that we cannot mean that God can do anything in the sense that for Him there is no difference between what is possible and what is impossible. There are certain things that God, being what He is, *cannot* do. God cannot do evil. Since He is love, He cannot act contrary to what love would dictate. Call this a limitation of His power, if you like. But in such limitation there is no defect, unless it be a defect in anyone that the better he is, the *less* capable he is of doing wrong. The defective character is that of the man who, as we say, "is capable of anything": you can never be sure what he will do next. God is not like that. It is just because of the perfection of His nature, that He cannot do everything. And, in fact, the Creed does not say that He can. The Greek word which is translated "Almighty" does not mean "able to do anything" but "all ruling" or "ruler of all things". God is the sole Ruler of the universe.

But if this is so—whence comes evil? Is its presence in the world compatible with belief in the sole rule of a God of love? The answer depends upon what we suppose to have been the purpose of God in creating the world. If, as the Christian believes, it was in order to produce beings capable of entering into fellowship with Him, and of returning love for love, that must involve in such beings at least a relative freedom and independence. It must involve, also, the possibility that we shall misuse the freedom God has given us—refuse the love which He asks from us, and choose what is evil instead of what is good. The real difficulty begins when we ask why we *should* choose evil; and it is here that the idea of a personal devil—a tempter—has always come in useful. But this idea, though superficially attractive, creates more difficulties than it solves. If we accept it, we come very near to supposing that God is *not* the sole ruler of the world—that He has a rival, and that He is really not omnipotent at all. It may well be that part of the reason for putting the word "Almighty" into the Creed, was to rule out the dualistic idea, that over against the good God there is an evil god, who is the source of the evil in the world.

But the question still remains—Why should man choose evil instead of good? For myself, I puzzled very much over this problem until I heard someone[1] offer a suggestion which, though not perhaps a complete solution, comes nearer it than any other I know. It was that selfishness is a necessary stage on the road to unselfishness. You must become aware of your selfhood before you can renounce it. Pride must come before humility. And therefore, this selfishness, which is the cause of most of the evil in the world, is the raw material of goodness. The advantage of this

[1]Professor C. E. Raven, sometime Dean of Emmanuel College.

suggestion is that it makes it possible to explain man's choice of evil, without bringing in an external tempter, and thus compromising God's omnipotence. However this may be, it seems to be clear that if man is to choose the right—fulfil the purpose for which God made him—it must be possible for him to choose the wrong, and thwart the purpose of God. That was "one of the necessary risks of a real creation". But it was a risk, it would seem, that God chose to take— and He took it, we must suppose, because He thought it worth taking. He had a purpose for us which could be achieved in no other way. And if we believe that that purpose is of all things most worth achieving, we cannot grumble at the conditions on which it depends. We cannot blame God for the evils which are caused by our misuse of our freedom. We cannot ask Him to take back from us His gift of freedom—to take from us the very thing that makes us men, and capable of becoming children of God—and we cannot ask Him to step in and put a stop to the evil which our misuse of that freedom produces.

Yet for one thing we can and must ask, and that is for some assurance that God can and will do something, consistent with retention of our freedom, to rescue us from the mess into which we have brought ourselves. And to that request Christianity gives no uncertain answer. It tells us that the power which gave us our freedom can conquer the evil which misuse of that freedom brings. And for proof it points us to the Cross of Christ; for there we see both the depth of God's love, and the final proof of His omnipotence. "It is impossible to assign limits to a power which can derive its very means of expression from that which checks it." So far from love and omnipotence being irreconcilable, it is impossible to conceive of any other omnipotence than the omnipotence of love. Archbishop Temple, in one of his sermons, contrasts the ease of Creation with the difficulty of Redemption. "The Creation is not the crowning achievement of God. Creation is easy: 'Let there be light, and there was light.' There is no resistance or disobedience. Creation was easy—but Redemption is infinitely difficult." It is in Redemption that God's power is seen, in the love which alone can win the final victory of free surrender of the human heart to that love. With our eyes on the Cross of Jesus, we can dare to declare our faith in a God who is both Father and Almighty.

5

I believe in God the Father Almighty, Maker of Heaven and Earth

God, as the Creed describes Him, is Father, Ruler and Creator. It is the idea of God as *Creator* that we are now to consider; and I am fully conscious of the inadequacy of what I have to say about it. We have seen that if we are to form any idea of God at all, we must use human analogies. Yet we need always to remember that the words we use to express our thought of God are analogies and no more. They can be true only in some more eminent sense beyond our understanding. And to remember this is particularly important when we speak of God as "Maker of heaven and earth". Anyone who has been to Chartres, will remember the sublime conception, on the south porch of the Cathedral, of the divine Sculptor moulding with loving care the half-formed figure of Adam. The thought of God as the Creator can perhaps best be expressed in terms of art and poetry. The danger begins when poetry is turned into prose. That is what has happened to the poetry of the first two chapters of Genesis. It has been understood as a literal account of the actual creation of the world. And in particular it has been inferred that the work of creation was completed, once and for all, at the beginning of time. "And the heavens and the earth were finished, and all the host of them. And on the seventh day God finished His work which He had made." That idea was corrected by St. John, when he put into the mouth of Jesus the words: "My Father is working still, and I am working" (Genesis ii: 1-2; John v: 17). But it still persists. And God is popularly supposed to have completed the work of creation, if not in 4004 B.C. at least at some time in the far distant past. The mistake comes from taking poetry for prose.

When we speak of God as Creator, we do not mean to say that God made the world as a watch maker makes a watch—turning it out of his workshop as a finished product. It is rather a symbolical expression of what we believe to be the permanent relation of God to the world, and to mankind in particular. "God is the ground and support of the world—not merely its beginning, for without Him it could not at any moment exist." The Christian doctrine of Creation has nothing whatever to do with the method by which the world has come into existence. It is a doctrine of the relationship to God of a world of things, and of a world of men. And the relationship to God of the world of men is, in an important sense, different from the relationship to Him of the world of things. Man, of course, is a part of nature. But he differs from the rest of nature in having a *personal* relation to God. That difference was expressed in Genesis, by saying that God made man in His own image. Man, though dependent on God for his existence, is sufficiently independent of God to be able to enter into personal relationship with Him, and indeed to co-operate with Him in the work of creation. He has been given a freedom that has been denied to the rest of nature.

At first sight, it is not quite easy to see how to hold together the two ideas of man's dependence on God, and his relative independence of Him. But it has been pointed out that some sort of human analogy may be found in the work of a novelist. The characters whom the novelist creates owe their existence to him. But, once created, they have a certain individuality and freedom of their own, and their creator cannot do what he likes with them. They must, in a sense, work out their own destinies. "We are frequently told by novelists," the Dean of St. Paul's has said, "that their characters have refused to fit into the scheme which had been prepared for them in advance." And this is borne out by Miss Dorothy Sayers, applying her experience as a novelist to problems of theology in her book *The Mind of the Maker*. "The free will," she says, "of a genuinely created character, has a certain reality which the writer will defy at his peril." To the kind of person who writes to her saying e.g., "Couldn't you make Lord Peter go to the Antarctic and investigate a murder on an exploring expedition?", she replies, "Leave my creature alone—I will not 'make' him do anything."

It is an obviously imperfect analogy. But it may help us to understand how God's human creatures, while dependent on Him for their existence, yet have a relative independence and freedom of their own. This freedom, as we know, they have misused. And while the story of the creation of man in Genesis symbolises his true relation to God, the story of man's fall symbolises his failure to realise that relation. No more than the creation story, is it a story of something that happened in the beginning of time. It is a symbol of man's failure to be what God meant him to be. And so God's work of creation is also a work of redemption. The two works cannot, in the end, be distinguished. The Creator is the Redeemer. As the Nicene Creed insisted, it was He "by whom all things were made: Who for us men and for our salvation came down from heaven." The God on whom the world depends for its existence is not a God who stands outside in passive contemplation of His world. He is a God who is actively engaged in the course of history—striving for the realisation of man's true relation to Him, for that "revelation of the sons of God" for which, as St. Paul says, "the whole creation waits in earnest expectation" (Romans viii: 19).

6

I believe in Jesus Christ His only Son our Lord

The Apostles' Creed begins with a declaration of
belief in God. But the Christian belief in God
depends upon the belief which comes second in the
Creed—belief "in Jesus Christ His only Son our
Lord".

That is the *heart* of the Creed—that from which
"the life-blood runs through all its arteries and veins
in constant movement—round and round, always
coming back to Him". I believe "in Jesus Christ His
only Son our Lord"—or, to put it the other way
round, "I believe in a God who is the Father of our
Lord Jesus Christ." To put it that way round helps
us, I think, to understand the true meaning of the
doctrine of the divinity of Christ. It is a doctrine
about *God*. It is better to say that God is Christ, than
to say that Christ is God. For to say that Christ is
God might suggest that apart from Christ we know
nothing about God at all. But that is plainly untrue.
After all, the Old Testament is a part of the Christian
Bible. "The invisible things of God," said St. Paul,
"since the creation of the world are clearly seen, being
perceived through the things that are made, even
His everlasting power and divinity" (Romans i:
20). There is a light which lights every man, even
those who have never heard of Christ. What the
Christian claims is that in Christ, as George Tyrrell

said, "these nebulous and scattered lights of revelation are gathered into a central sun". In Christ, God and His purpose are made plain. Christ is the key, by which the secrets of the universe are unlocked. *That* the Christian must believe, or he has no right to the name of Christian. But it is only in a lesser degree, I would suggest, that he is required to accept any particular explanation of this belief.

Now there are two facts about Jesus which any explanation must take into account. The first is that He was a *man*. Any explanation of Jesus must start from the solid fact of His humanity. But if it must start there, it cannot end there. For if the humanity of Jesus is certain, no less certain is the fact that Christians have found *God* in Christ. "Come unto me, all ye that labour and are heavy laden . . . and ye shall find rest unto your souls" (Matthew xi: 28, 29). To the truth of that claim, the history of Christianity bears witness. Christians have found in Christ what could only be found in God. They know that He can do what only God could do. It was its conviction of the truth of these two facts about Jesus, which led the Church at the Council of Chalcedon in A.D. 451 to formulate the doctrine of the two natures in Christ. "Our Lord Jesus Christ," so the statement of the Council ran, "is one and the same Son, the same perfect in deity, the same perfect in humanity . . . truly God and truly Man . . . to be acknowledged in two natures without confusion . . . the distinction of natures being in no way removed in consequence of the union, but rather the special character of each nature being preserved and concurring in one Person." Now I think it is clear that that is not really an explanation, but simply a statement of the facts that are to be explained. Yet an explanation is certainly needed. How can one individual have two natures? You cannot separate nature from personality in that way. The fact is that those who drew up that statement were hampered by an inadequate idea of human nature. Leo, Bishop of Rome, in a letter which was accepted as authoritative at the Council, was able to say that "to be hungry, to be thirsty, to be weary, and to sleep, are evidently human". Well, so they are; but they are not characteristically human. The true nature of man is not to be found in characteristics which he shares with animals, but in those moral and spiritual characteristics which differentiate him from animals, and make him worthy to be called a child of God. The humanity of Jesus does not, therefore, rule out the possibility that He was, as human, an incarnation of the Divine.

Yet there is something which differentiates Jesus from ordinary men. What is it? It seems to me that here St. Paul can help us. Christian experience has found in Jesus a strange combination of individuality and universality. On the one hand, He was a real individual man. Christians have often tended to overlook this. They have preferred to speak of Him as *Man* rather than *a* man. But in recent years the balance has been redressed. The lives of Jesus which have poured from the Press are not all of equal value, but the best of them have made Jesus live again for us, with a vividness of colour that we had never before imagined. I shall never forget my first reading of T. R. Glover's *The Jesus of History*. Jesus was a real man, with an intense individuality of His own. But there is also something universal about

Him. Has any other man ever had the power which Jesus has to draw to Himself the devotion of men of all types, of all races, of all ages? He was a man, but He was also humanity. He was, in fact, "the Man in men, become a man". And that was how St. Paul thought of Him. In Jesus we see the "image of God" in which man was made—we see humanity as God intended it to be. The splendour of God, which man was meant to reflect, was seen in the face of Christ. All through its history—so St. Paul believed—the human race had drawn its spiritual life from Christ. The children of Israel in the wilderness "drank of the spiritual Rock that followed them, and the Rock was Christ" (1 Corinthians x: 4). What happened when Jesus was born into the world, was that this Christ, He who is always and everywhere the "Man in men", became *a* man.

And there is something else that we can learn from St. Paul. It was what Christ had *done* and could do for Paul that was the basis of his faith in Him. People have often sought other grounds on which to base their faith in Christ—the manner of His birth, His miracles, His sayings about Himself. St. Paul based everything on the saving power of Christ. And that is a firm foundation for faith. "I live", he could say, "yet not I, but Christ lives in me; and the life which I now live in the flesh, I live by virtue of my faith in the Son of God, who loved me and gave Himself for me" (Galatians ii: 20). How can you explain such an experience except as St. Paul explained it—that "God was in Christ, reconciling the world unto Himself" (2 Corinthians v: 19)?

7

Who was conceived by the Holy Ghost, born of the Virgin Mary

We come now to what is perhaps the most controversial statement in the whole Creed—and I can hardly expect that all will agree with what I have to say about it. "Who was conceived by the Holy Ghost, born of the Virgin Mary." The inclusion of these words in the Creed would seem to imply that the story of the miraculous birth of Jesus, as told in the Gospels of Matthew and Luke, is to be accepted as an essential part of the Christian faith; and that is something which many people at the present day will not allow. Not only do they doubt the truth of the story—they do not *want* it to be true. What are we to say about it? Well, first, what is the evidence for it? The story is told in the Gospels of Matthew and Luke, which were written probably some eighty years after the birth of Jesus. There is no mention of it in our earliest Gospel, nor anywhere else in the New Testament. Of course that does not prove that the other writers did not know of it, or did not accept it as true. But it is strange that if they did know of it, they should have made no use of it in support of their teaching about Jesus—especially strange in the case of the writer of the fourth Gospel. For he deliberately undertook, as he tells us, to show that "Jesus is the Christ, the Son of God". And therefore, if he never

mentions the Virgin Birth, we must assume either
that he was not aware of it, or at least that he attached
no apologetic value to it. He did not regard it as
necessary for the purpose of proving that "Jesus is the
Christ, the Son of God". How we are to account for
the origin of the story, if we suppose that it was not
based on fact, it is hard to say. But the idea of the
Spirit as active in creation might have had something
to do with it. Just as the Spirit was at work at the
foundation of the world (the Spirit of God "brooding
upon the face of the waters"), so the inauguration of
God's new creation might have been ascribed to the
activity of the same Spirit. And in a Hellenistic
environment—though hardly in a Jewish one—that
might have led to such a story as we find in Matthew
and Luke. However, the point at the moment is that
the historical evidence for the Virgin Birth is incon-
clusive. A modern historian of Christian doctrine has
given it as his opinion that it is equally impossible to
prove the tradition true, or to prove it false, and that
belief in it depends on other considerations than those
of historical evidence.

Now, it has been maintained that there *are* such
considerations. The idea that birth through His
mother alone was a necessary condition of the sin-
lessness of Jesus, is one which we need hardly consider today. But we cannot ignore the widely held
opinion that the Virgin Birth of Christ, if not necessary to belief in His divinity, at least lends strong support to that belief. And this it is, I think, which
makes people unwilling to question the truth of the
Virgin Birth. It is not merely because it is in the Bible
and in the Creed, but, above all, because they think
that without it the divinity of Christ becomes some-

how less certain. I can sympathise with their fears, but I am sure they are unfounded. As I have already suggested, belief in the divinity of Christ springs from the Christian experience of His saving power, a power which belongs to God alone—-an experience to which all Christian history bears witness. And if that is true, it follows that, as proof of His divinity, the manner of His birth is quite irrelevant. However He was born, the fact of His saving power remains. And no belief about His birth can either throw doubt on that, or give support to it. Christian experience has shown that He can do what God alone could do—that He can supply the "bread of life", and that in Him men can find rest for their souls. It has sometimes been maintained that His miraculous birth was at least a fitting prelude to the earthly life of the Saviour of the world. But was His crucifixion as a criminal, in that sense, a "fitting" end to His life? He "emptied Himself," said St. Paul. And is it not reasonable to suppose that self-emptying began from His very birth itself? However that may be, what I think we must insist upon is, that fitting or unfitting, the Virgin Birth of Christ has no bearing on the truth of His divinity. A modern theologian has said that "the Virgin Birth, if it could be historically proved, would be no demonstration of Christ's divinity, nor would the disproof of it throw any doubt upon that doctrine". And with that I think we must agree.

Yet, when we have said all this, we cannot but ask whether, neverthless, the idea of the Virgin Birth may not have value for Christians. We can't altogether ignore the fact that at least from the second century the belief in it has formed part of the Christian tradition, and that it has been given a place in the Creed.

We must recognise also the religious significance which generations of Christians have found in it. It has drawn to itself the devotion of Christian people all down the ages. It has inspired some of the most perfect expressions of the art of painter and poet, sculptor and glass-painter. Must there not be some value to be found in it somewhere? Here it is in the Creed—but for many people that is a serious difficulty. Is it not dishonest to confess your belief in something, about the truth of which you are, at least, doubtful? About this I would say two things.

(1) In repeating the Creed, we are not giving our intellectual assent to certain doctrines. We are confessing our faith in God, as Christ has revealed Him; and that revelation did not take the form of a system of doctrine, but of a human life. At the heart of the Christian religion we find not a philosophy but a story. It gives us "truth embodied in a tale". Of that the yearly round of Church worship is a continual reminder, recounting over and over again "the old, old story of Jesus and His love". Even the Creed itself takes, for the most part, the form of a story. In repeating it, we are confessing our faith in the God who so revealed Himself—in the God who "so loved the world that He gave His only begotten Son" for its salvation. Within this larger context, the clause about the Virgin Birth of Christ takes only a subordinate place. Doubt as to its historical accuracy need not prevent us from using the Creed as a confession of our whole-hearted faith in that great act of God of which the story tells.

(2) In every clause of the Creed, what matters, as I have said before, is not the literal statement, but "the religious conviction, the spiritual reality to

which the literal statement points". And in this case, the spiritual reality is surely the belief that in Christ something *new* came into the world, something like a new creation took place. Humanity made a fresh beginning. Into a broken and despairing world, God had brought new life. What man could not do, God had done. That was the reality which belief in the Virgin Birth mediated. And if we should not inter-pret our experience of this reality in the same way, yet the same experience may be ours. "God so loved the world, that He gave His only begotten Son." If we believe that, then we share the conviction which belief in the Virgin Birth of Christ helped to sustain.

8

Suffered under Pontius Pilate, Was crucified, dead and buried

The Creed contains a date. That is a startling and tremendously important fact. Christianity rests on the belief that history reveals God. The elaborate dating with which Luke opens his account of the ministry of Jesus has been judged to be one of the most significant things in the New Testament. Christianity is not a system of truths, which, once they have been enunciated, can (as it were) stand up on their own feet, independently of the person who uttered them. Christianity is bound up with a Person who lived in Palestine in the first century, and the approximate date of whose death is important enough to be mentioned in the Creed. It is the historical nature of Christianity which lies behind the idea of Apostolic succession, the use of old historic creeds in Church worship in spite of difficulties which such use presents to people of a later age, the importance which is attached to New Testament criticism, and the immense labour devoted to recovery of the true text of the New Testament. Above all, perhaps, it is to be seen in the yearly commemoration of the Gospel story in Church worship. From Christmas to Passiontide and Easter, over and over again "the old, old story" is told. Week by week or day by day, the saving work of Christ is proclaimed in the Eucharist, and we find ourselves in imagination in the upper room on the night in which Jesus was betrayed. Christianity is a historic religion. It rests on the belief that God acts in history—that events reveal Him, and that He was supremely revealed in certain events which took place in Palestine in the first century.

Let us consider how this applies to the story of the Passion. As we read the story in the Gospels, it becomes clear that it is told from two different points of view. It has a double aspect; and to appreciate this is the first step towards understanding it. On the one hand, the crucifixion of Jesus is a fact of history. And we can form a reasonably clear idea of why, on the historical plane, it happened. The ruling class in Palestine recognised in Jesus a disturbing and dangerous influence. The story of the Passion begins with the account of a plot of the chief priests and scribes, who decide that Jesus must be put to death quickly and secretly. The motives which united the priests and scribes in opposition to Jesus were not the same. The priests were the aristocracy of Jerusalem; they were die-hard conservatives, who distrusted novelties of any kind; and Jesus was a dangerous novelty. The scribes, and the party of the Pharisees with which they were closely associated, opposed Jesus from a higher motive. They could not condone what they regarded as His violation of the Law. To put conscience before Law, as He did, was subversive of the very foundations of religion. Moreover, the ordinary people, who at one time "heard Him gladly", had become disillusioned by His failure to be and do what they had expected of Him. And in the circle of His own disciples, there was not only misunderstanding but treachery. Given all that, the end was inevitable. That is the human side of the story.

But there is another side to it. Underlying the story as the Gospels tell it is the conviction that the death of Jesus was not a mere martyrdom or a mere miscarriage of justice. The words which St. John put into the mouth of Jesus only make explicit what is implied by the memorable story as told in all the four Gospels. "No man taketh my life from Me, but I lay it down of Myself" (John x: 18). He deliberately challenges the authorities by going up to Jerusalem—because, as He said, "I have a baptism to be baptised with" (Luke xii: 50). As the story of Gethsemane tells, He went to His death in the certainty that it was the will of God—and went to meet it determined that God's will should be done. And the only explanation of His strange silence before Pilate, and apparent refusal to clear Himself of the obviously false accusation brought against Him, is that the whole affair was to Him of no moment at all. He had already devoted His life, and what the Roman Procurator could do was only the appointed way by which this self-devotion was to be carried into effect. Schweitzer (in *The Quest of the Historical Jesus*) spoke of Him as "the one immeasurably great Man, who was strong enough to think of Himself as the spiritual ruler of mankind and to bend history to His purpose". The Son of Man must suffer. That at least is what the Gospels suggest. The Crucifixion happened (as Peter said on the day of Pentecost) "by the appointed will and foreknowledge of God" (Acts ii: 23).

There are then two sides to the story of the Crucifixion—two aspects from which we may look at it— and we must not confuse them: (1) the human aspect, which we can explain as the result of actions of men, whose motives we can identify: we can see why it happened, and why, humanly speaking, it must have happened; and (2) the divine aspect. It would be wrong to think of Jesus as having come into the world in order to be crucified. To put it crudely, we can hardly think of God, as it were, engineering the crucifixion of Jesus. But nevertheless, it is true that what gives significance to the death of Jesus, is the divine purpose which underlies it. It was the result of the action of *God*, working through One who was completely in harmony with His purpose. There is this other and quite different sense in which it *must* have happened. The Crucifixion is an event in history. It happened in Palestine in the early years of the first century; and we can trace the historical causes which led to it. But it is more than an event in history. It is a revelation of what always happens when God meets evil. "As the flash of the volcano discloses for a few hours the elemental fires at the

B*

earth's centre, so the light on Calvary was the bursting forth through historical conditions of the very nature of the Everlasting." Even that simile is not quite adequate. The Passion of Christ is not merely a revelation of God's nature. In it we see God in action. That is what gives finality to it. God did something then which can never, and need never, be repeated. And that is why we find included in the Creed the plain historical statement (without any theological interpretation) that Jesus Christ, whom we have already confessed as God's only Son, our Lord, was "crucified, dead, and buried".

9

He descended into hell

These words were a late insertion into the original Creed, and their first appearance was in a Creed of the middle of the fourth century. Yet they seem to represent a very early belief. Very soon the question must have been asked: "What happened to Jesus in the interval between His death and His resurrection on the third day?" And the answer that seems to have been given was that He went to the place where all the dead go. St. Peter, in his speech on the day of Pentecost, said that David in Psalm 16 had foreseen the resurrection of Christ, when he said, "Thou wilt not leave my soul in Hades" (Acts ii: 31). In St. Matthew's Gospel it is said that Jesus refused to give any sign to those who asked for one "except the sign of Jonah"—and added: "For as Jonah was three days and three nights in the belly of the whale, so shall the Son of Man be three days and three nights in the heart of the earth" (Matthew xii: 40). And perhaps that is the way in which the words of Jesus to the dying thief were understood: "Today thou shalt be with me in Paradise." Jesus, like all who die, went, it was believed, to the abode of the dead. And these words may have been put into the Creed partly to express the faith that in death as in life He was man, and what happens to all who die happened to Him: "he descended into Hades"—into the abode of the dead. In that case, the presence of these words in the Creed is not without its value.

What happens to us after death, must always be (despite the claims of the Spiritualist) a matter of faith, and not of exact knowledge. But there are two reasons, at least, which make it natural for us to believe in some kind of "intermediate state"—some time of waiting after death. (1) The Christian believes that the purpose of his life here on earth is to acquire the knowledge of God, which is eternal life. We have no right to presume that those who waste their opportunities here will be given a second chance. Yet when this life ends, even the most promising pupil would have to confess that he still had much to learn. And if there are few of us who are bad enough for hell, there must be even fewer who are good enough for heaven. We seem bound to suppose that in the life beyond there will be opportunity for further progress—what Origen called "some place of instruction", or as it were a class-room or school of souls. (2) And there is perhaps another reason for supposing that there must be a time of waiting after death. If it is true that salvation of the individual depends upon the salvation of society, then it would seem to follow that "apart from us they (the dead) should not be made perfect" (Hebrews xi: 40). God has prepared some "far-off divine event, to which the whole creation moves". And the salvation of the individual must wait upon the fulfilment of His purpose for the world. If all this is true, then we may be thankful that our Creed allows us to believe that Jesus Himself passed through the stage of waiting, through which we must all pass, and consecrated by His presence the condition of departed souls. So that with a confidence far beyond the reach of the Psalmist we can say: "Though I walk through the valley of the shadow of death, I will fear no evil, for Thou art with me."

But it appears that the early Christians were not content to believe that Jesus went to the abode of the dead. They wanted to know what He did there. As early as the second century, it was believed that He went to preach the Gospel to the saints of the Old Testament and rescue them from the domain of death. This idea is reflected in the form in which this clause appears in a Creed of the fourth century: "Who also went down into the nether world, and when the gate-keepers of Hades saw Him, they shuddered." And a Christian writer of the second century (Justin Martyr) quotes what he calls a prophecy of Jeremiah: "The Lord, the God of Israel, remembered His dead, who were asleep in the earth which was their tomb, and He descended to preach to them His salvation." I think we must at least recognise that this was a praiseworthy attempt to find an answer to a problem which is with us still. What may we suppose to be the destiny of those who have never had an opportunity to become acquainted with the revelation of God in Christ? Those, in particular, who, living before Christ came, made the most of such opportunities as they had, yet never knew God's supreme revelation of Himself? If it is true that there is not "any other name under heaven, that is given among men, wherein we must be saved" (Acts iv: 12), must we suppose that those who have never heard of that Name are debarred thereby from salvation? The answer that was given does not go far enough, it was too narrowly Jewish in its outlook. Yet at least those who made it were feeling after the idea of the universality of the Gospel. Christ is the Light of the World, "the true light which lighteth every man". And as the writer of the fourth Gospel said, before the Word became flesh, He was in the world (John i. 10). He who became flesh in Jesus of Nazareth is the source of all that is good and true in every age and among all peoples. There is a sense in which we can say that there were Christians before Christ, and Christians who have never heard of Christ. The Spirit of Christ is not bound.

We have seen that the question which we have to ask about each clause in the Creed is: What is the religious conviction, the spiritual reality, to which the literal statement points? I hope I have shown that the religious conviction which led to the inclusion in the Creed of the words "He descended into hell" is one which every Christian may and must share.

10

The third day He rose again from the dead

In form, the words are a pure statement of fact. But they owe their place in the Creed, of course, to the belief that that fact had a vital significance for faith. About this, as about all clauses in the Creed, we have to ask: What is the religious conviction, the spiritual reality, to which the literal statement points? And the answer, I think, is not quite so simple as is often supposed.

First, as to the fact. Let us imagine that we have gone to the theatre, to see a three-act play. The first act of this play begins in the Garden of Gethsemane. Jesus is arrested—and the disciples "all left Him and fled", so Mark tells us. In his Gospel that is the last we hear of them—except for Peter, who followed Jesus, but only to disown his acquaintance with Him. The curtain falls on the scene of the Crucifixion. "At the end of the first Good Friday, there remained only one loyal Christian in the world, and He was apparently dead." (But we have had to leave the theatre during the second act of the play, and we return in time for the third.)

The scene of the third act is laid some few weeks later in Jerusalem—the very place where Jesus had been crucified and His body buried. Peter is addressing a crowd. His speech works up to a climax. "Let all the house of Israel know assuredly, that God hath

made Him both Lord and Christ—this Jesus whom
ye crucified" (Acts ii: 36). The Christian Church,
founded on that assurance is already in existence.
What has happened in the second act? Something
must have happened to make the third act possible.
Somehow or other, what had looked like defeat was
now seen to be victory. Something had produced
this change. And "no event," it has been said, "was
ever witnessed to by such a change from defeat to
triumph, and by such long and unswerving devotion
in lives that showed the power of the belief as well as
the conviction of it". That is the conclusion to which
we are driven, without having seen the second act
of the play.

So we go and buy a copy of the complete play and
read the second act. And we ought, I think, to be a
little surprised at what we read. Does it really explain
the third act? There is a visit to the tomb in the early
hours of Sunday morning by some women who fail
to find what they are looking for. There are several
scenes depicting appearances of Jesus to His disciples,
who are convinced that He is alive. But that is not
enough, we say to ourselves. Of course it is not. And
our mistake today, and the cause of much of our
confusion, is to suppose that it *is* enough, and that if
we could get conclusive proof of the fact of the empty
tomb and of the reality of the appearances of Jesus,
we should have established the truth of the belief on
which Christianity rests. But that belief was not, and is
not, simply that Jesus had risen from the dead. It was
that "God had made Him both Lord and Christ". And
no amount of proof that His tomb was empty, and that
He was alive, could of itself establish His divinity.

Now, it is significant that it is only the disciples who

are said to have seen the risen Jesus. That need not mean that there was really nothing to see, and that what they thought they saw was just the product of their imagination. The beauty of a picture is none the less real because it is visible only to the eye of the expert. But it does mean that what they saw was not so obvious that no one còuld help seeing it. Most people did not see it, and were unconvinced by the disciples' story of what they had seen. It was extraordinary and unaccountable if true. But it *meant* something only to those whose eyes had been opened to see the reality of which it was the outward and visible sign. It was a reality which only faith can see. What that reality was, is perhaps most clearly brought out in the fourth Gospel. The writer makes it clear that the Crucifixion was not just a disaster which was "reversed" by the Resurrection. The report of the Church of England Commission on Christian Doctrine, published some years ago, spoke of the Resurrection as having "reversed the Crucifixion". There is a sense, no doubt, in which this is true. The purpose of those who crucified Jesus was frustrated. Defeat was turned into victory. But to think of the Resurrection as "reversing" the Crucifixion is misleading, in so far as it implies that the work which Jesus had accomplished was unfinished and incomplete. According to St. John, Jesus had said: "My meat is to do the will of Him that sent me, and to accomplish His work." And St. John tells us also that His last words were: "It is finished." His work had been done. There was nothing more for Him to do. "Lifted up from the earth", he would "draw all men to Himself" (John iv: 34, xix: 30, xii: 32). His defeat *was* His victory.

That was the reality of which the Resurrection was the sign. The Resurrection faith was the conviction that the death of Christ was not a disaster, but a revelation of the heart of God. Perhaps we do not realise as we should how extraordinary it was that the disciples should have come to see the death of Jesus in that light—should have seen it, not as one would have expected they would, as a defeat of God's purpose and a denial of His love, but the final proof of His love. "God," said St. Paul, "commendeth *His own* love towards us, in that while we were yet sinners, Christ died for us" (Romans v: 8). God was in Christ, and never more clearly so than in His death on the Cross. "There was a light on Calvary, and that light was the bursting forth through historical conditions of the very nature of the Everlasting." There is a sense in which it is true to say that the Christian faith rests entirely on the truth of the Resurrection—and that, therefore, it is the most fundamental of all Christian beliefs. But that does not mean that we can prove the truth of Christianity by establishing the fact of the empty tomb, or that our faith in Christ depends upon that fact. It depends rather upon the facts of Christian experience as a whole. And of those facts the most fundamental is the most universal—the experience of all those who in presence of Christ crucified have been moved to exclaim: "My Lord and my God."

The verification of the story cannot of itself produce the faith which the disciples based on it. We must see what they saw. We, too, must stand before the Cross of Jesus. And if, as we stand there, we hear God speaking to us, and know that to turn away would be to refuse the light and choose the darkness, then we shall begin to understand what the disciples meant when they declared that Christ was risen from the dead.

11

*He ascended into Heaven, And sitteth on the right hand of
God the Father Almighty*

Of all the articles of the Creed there is none, perhaps, that is both so important and so misunderstood as this one. The traditional picture of the Ascension, as it appears in Christian art, is based on the story told by Luke at the beginning of Acts. That story is part and parcel of what I think we must call St. Luke's peculiar idea of the Resurrection. His description of the Resurrection appearances (Luke xxiv: 36-43) suggests that he thought of the Resurrection as at least a partial return of Jesus to earth. And that made it necessary for him to explain how this quasi-physical sojourn of the risen Christ on earth was brought to an end. It had to be assumed that one of those appearances was the last, and that somehow this fact was made clear to the disciples.

We cannot tell what the origin of this story may have been. But it is certain that nowhere else in the New Testament is this idea of the Resurrection to be found, and nowhere else the story which was its necessary corollary. Elsewhere the Resurrection is not a return of Jesus to earth, but is itself His exaltation from earth to heaven. St. Paul can write to the

Colossians (iii:1): "If you then were raised together with Christ, seek the things that are above, where Christ is seated on the right hand of God." And similarly for St. John the Resurrection is the exaltation of Christ. That we should recover this idea of the Resurrection seems to me to be very important. It is not the view which has prevailed in the Church. The Church has accepted St. Luke's idea of the Resurrection, and with it, as its necessary sequel, his story of the Ascension. It is significant that the Prayer Book on Ascension Day has to turn to Acts for its Epistle, and to the certainly unauthentic ending of Mark for its Gospel. And it is not perhaps surprising that Ascension Day should be so little observed by people who find Luke's story something of a stumbling block.

Now, I think it would be true to say that the doctrine of the Ascension is the most fundamental of all Christian doctrines; but its truth is quite independent of the story with which it has been associated. Belief in the Ascension was a belief which grew inevitably out of the experience of the first Christians. We find it closely associated with the coming of the Spirit. The writer of the Epistle to the Ephesians pictures Christ as a conqueror in a triumphal procession, giving gifts to His people: "When He ascended on high, He led captivity captive, and gave gifts unto men." The gift of the Spirit could only have been possible if Christ had "ascended far above all the heavens, that He might fill all things" (Ephesians iv: 8-10). And in the fourth Gospel the idea runs through the discourses of Jesus at the Last Supper that "it is expedient that He should *go away*", for only on that condition could the Spirit come. During

His earthly life Christ was confined, circumscribed and limited. If He was to "fill all things", He must be set free from the limitations of earthly existence.

It is clear, then, that belief in the Ascension was not really based on the idea that Jesus was literally carried heavenwards by a cloud. It was based on the experience of His spiritual presence. The only adequate explanation of that experience was that "He had ascended into heaven, and was sitting on the right hand of God the Father Almighty". That, of course, is metaphorical language—of a kind that was natural to those who thought of God as living in an unknown and mysterious region above the solid vault of the sky. The idea becomes more intelligible to us if we translate it into a different metaphor. There is scriptural authority for thinking of God as the Light of the World. He is the Source from which the world draws all the light it has. He is its Sun. It is less true to think of the light of God as in the world, than to think of the world as in the light of God—as the earth is in the light of the sun. And the relation between earth and heaven can, therefore, be compared to the relation between the earth and the sun. The Christian belief in the Ascension is, therefore, belief that *Christ* is the Light of the World. Christians were led to that conviction by the experience of the power of Christ in their lives, of that gift of the Spirit which could come from no other source than from One who (in the metaphorical language of the Creed) "sitteth on the right hand of God the Father Almighty", One who "had ascended far above all the heavens, that He might fill all things". And that, too, was the real basis of belief in the Resurrection. The two beliefs are complementary: you cannot believe in one without the other. But of the two, the belief in the Ascension is the more fundamental. As I have tried to show, the disciples' faith in Christ could not have been based simply on the fact of the disappearance of the body of Jesus from the tomb, and His appearance to His disciples, however certain those facts might have been. But we can put it the other way round, and say that to people who were so vividly conscious of the love and power of Christ in their lives, belief in His Resurrection would be inevitable. And, therefore, I would say that the real basis of their faith, including their belief in the Resurrection, was the (for them) unquestionable fact of the Ascension. But the certainty of that fact did not depend on the story which Luke tells at the beginning of the Acts. No one, indeed, but he appealed to it. It depended on the conviction that only One who "had ascended far above all the heavens" could be the Bread of Life and the Light of the World—all that in their experience they had found Christ to be.

12

From thence He shall come to judge the quick and the dead

(a)

This clause in the Creed contains two points, which can, I think, best be treated separately. It will be convenient to consider it in two instalments, and to take first the belief in what is called the

"Second Coming" of Christ, and second the idea of the "Judgment".

First, then, the "Second Coming". That the first Christians lived in daily expectation of the return of Christ, there can be no doubt. "The Lord Himself," wrote St. Paul to the Thessalonians, "shall descend from heaven with a shout, with the voice of the archangel, and with the trump of God, and the dead in Christ shall rise first; then we that are alive . . . shall together with them be caught up in the clouds to meet the Lord." (1 Thess. iv: 16, 17). Christ would return in the life time of that generation. Whether there was any authority for this expectation in the teaching of Jesus Himself, is a matter of which we cannot be so sure. At least His ethical teaching seems to imply that He believed that human society would continue in a form in which such teaching would not cease to be relevant. It cannot really be explained, as has sometimes been suggested, as having been designed only for a short period which must elapse before His return. However that may be, the first Christians undoubtedly looked for the immediate return of Christ, and with it the end of the present age—though later New Testament writers were not so sure. Anyhow, the expectation was not fulfilled. We must conclude that it was based on a misapprehension.

But it does not follow that it did not arise from a true insight into the meaning of the Christian revelation. The first Christians expected the end of "the present age"—the end of history. But what is meant by the "end of history?" If you think of history as a succession of events, then the "Last Things" (the things with which eschatology is concerned) will be things that happen at the end of history so understood. But if you think of history as the Jew thought of it, as the working out of God's purpose, then the Last Things may be said to take place when that purpose is finally revealed. And throughout the New Testament there runs the belief that the End in that sense had come. That being so, it was natural to suppose that the end of history in a temporal sense must at least be near at hand. Time proved that this expectation was mistaken; but that did not matter. Christianity survived the non-fulfilment of the hope of Christ's immediate return. That is of immense significance, for it shows that that hope was not really fundamental. If it had been, Christianity could not have survived its non-fulfilment.

But it was *not* fundamental. The fundamental belief concerned, not the future, but the present. It was that in Jesus the final purpose of God had been revealed, and His victory over the powers of evil had been won. Yet, of course—and here we come to the point—there was a sense in which the victory was still to be won. The powers of evil were still active. The rule of God was not yet complete. It was equally true, both that the End had come, and that the End was still to come. You could say "Thine is the Kingdom", but you must also pray "Thy Kingdom come". It was this double truth which was expressed in the idea of the *return* of Christ. The long-expected Messiah had come, and with Him the Kingdom of God. Yet there was a sense in which the Kingdom was still in the future. We can explain the hope of the return of Christ as an attempt to express this double truth. It stood for the "completion of that which was already final". If that sounds somewhat paradoxical, I suggest that an analogy

may be found in war. Isn't it true that often the final
decisive battle is fought long before the war is over?
The End has come, and yet it has not come. No doubt
this was not the way in which the first Christians
thought of the return of Christ. They expected a
literal return, and with it the end of history. It was
natural to mistake symbol for reality; and of course
there are many who do so still. But the symbol expresses a conviction about the present rather than
about the future. It expresses the belief that in Christ
the victory of God has been won—that the decisive
battle has been fought, and therefore the end of the
war is certain, however long it may go on.

It follows that attempts which have continually
been made to foretell the end of the world, and cal-
culate the date when it will take place are, from the
Christian standpoint, altogether misguided. The
Christian—quâ Christian—has no interest in such
speculations. Indeed, the End, as the Christian
understands it, is not in itself an event in history at
all, which can be calculated and dated. The End,
like the beginning, lies outside history. As C. H. Dodd
has said—the coming of Christ, and the final victory
of God's rule "is not itself an event like other events
in history, but in some sense a reality transcending
history". It is the point at which *all* history is taken
up into the larger whole of God's eternal purpose.
That purpose was revealed in Christ. And belief in
the second coming of Christ, rightly understood,
arises inevitably out of a true understanding of the
significance of His first coming. It is true that we can
no longer look for a literal return of Christ upon the
clouds. Yet we can, and must, believe the truth which
that hope was an attempt to express—that it is the

age-long purpose of God to "sum up all things in Christ" (Ephesians i: 10). That, I would suggest, is the "religious conviction, the spiritual reality", to which the literal statement of this clause of the Creed points—and to which we give our assent when we say the Creed.

13

From thence He shall come to judge the quick and the dead

(b)

We have considered the Christian belief in the Second Coming of Christ. Our subject now is that which, according to the Creed, is the purpose of that coming: "to judge the quick and the dead". The thought of the Last Judgment inevitably, perhaps, calls up before our minds a picture of the Great Assize—so often depicted in stone or glass at the west end of medieval Churches—the scene described in the Revelation of St. John, of "the great white throne, and Him that sat upon it . . . the dead, the great and the small, stood before the throne, and the books were opened . . . and if any was not found written in the book of life, he was cast into the lake of fire" (Revelation xx: 11-15). I suppose that today most of us would recognise that the value of that picture is to be found in the truth which it symbolises, and that it is not to be understood as a literal description of a future event. But what does it symbolise? What is the truth to which it points?

I have suggested that the real purpose of the belief in the Second Coming of Christ is to express a conviction about the present rather than about the future. It would seem to follow that the same must be true of this closely related belief in the Last Judgment. And this, in fact, is what we find plainly stated in the fourth Gospel. St. Paul has said that "we shall all stand before the judgment seat of Christ" (2 Corinthians v: 10). According to St. John, we stand already before that judgment seat. "For judgment [the Christ can say] am I come into this world." "This is the judgment, that the light is come into the world, and men loved the darkness rather than the light" (John ix: 39, iii: 19). That was not a fanciful theory, but a statement of actual experience. Those who came into contact with Christ, and those who heard of Him through others, were conscious of His judgment upon them. "Depart from me, for I am a sinful man, O Lord" (Luke v: 8). And this judgment resulted in a separation (that is the literal meaning of the word translated "judgment") between those who acknowledged the truth of Christ's judgment upon them, and accepted His forgiveness, and those who did not acknowledge it—who saw the light, and rejected it. By their response to the light, men pronounce their own judgment. I would suggest that the purpose of the idea of the Last Judgment is to express the *finality* of this separation—to give a symbolical picture of the truth that our attitude to Christ is determinative of our eternal destiny.

It is significant that in the picture of the Great Assize the Judge is Christ. (Matthew xxv: 31ff.) That symbolises the eternal significance, "for us men and for our salvation", of *Christ*. We make, as I believe, a serious mistake if we "objectivise", as it were, the symbolism of the Last Judgment—if we substitute finality in time for finality in significance. However, if there is truth in all this, it confronts us with a problem of great difficulty. If Christ, and our attitude to Christ, is of such central importance, what of those who have never heard of Him—who lived before His time or have never come within reach of His influence? Can they be judged by their attitude to One whom they have never known? Now, I think St. Paul has something to say which may help us here, and point a way out of the difficulty. St. Paul spoke of Christ as the "Second Adam". From Him he believed that the human race had always drawn its spiritual life. He said that the children of Israel "drank of the spiritual Rock that followed them, and the Rock was Christ" (1 Corinthians x: 4). What did he mean by that? Well—perhaps he was feeling after the idea that the Jesus of history was the incarnation of the eternal Christ—that He who was born into this world was none other than He from whom man has always drawn his spiritual life, and that therefore even those who had lived before His incarnation had in some real sense known Him. The writer of the fourth Gospel expressed the same thought when he said that He who became flesh in Jesus of Nazareth was the Word who had always been, in the world which He had made, the "Light which lights every man" (John i: 9, 10). And it would seem to follow that even those who have never heard of the historical Jesus may in some way have been confronted by the eternal Christ, and judged by their response to His light—that light that they have seen.

There is a further point to remember. It is surely

true that what God requires of us is not that we should attain to some absolute standard of perfection, but that we should make the most of such opportunities as we have. The greater the opportunity, the higher the standard that is required. "Unto whomsoever much is given, of him shall much be required." But there is a light that lights *every man*; and those who have responded to the spark of light that they have seen are surely more fit for heaven than those who have seen a more brilliant light, but have not responded to it. This is not to say that the knowledge of the Jesus of the Gospels is superfluous—or that the Christian missionary is wasting his time. That would imply that the Incarnation might as well never have happened. But at least we have no right to say that men who have never heard of Jesus of Nazareth are outside the pale of salvation. That is surely to set unwarrantable limits to the working of God's grace. Yet for the Christian it remains true that Christ is the Judge, that His is the standard of judgment; and belief in the "Last Judgment" is belief in the *finality* of that judgment. By our attitude to the Christ we have seen, we are judged. "This is the judgment, that the Light is come into the world." Our eternal destiny depends upon our response to that Light.

14

I believe in the Holy Ghost

(a)

We come now to the third division of the Creed, which begins "I believe in the Holy Ghost". There is no part of Christian doctrine, I suppose, which has remained so ill-defined and undeveloped as belief in the Holy Spirit. Yet for the understanding and interpretation of Christianity in the world of today, it is peculiarly important.

Our natural starting-point is the account in Acts of what is sometimes called the "descent" of the Spirit at Pentecost. As the Proper Preface for Whit Sunday in the Prayer Book puts it: "According to Christ's most true promise, the Holy Ghost came down as at this time from heaven." *Came down.* It is, of course, a metaphor, but it is a somewhat misleading metaphor. For the essence of belief in the Spirit is precisely the belief that God does not need to come down, as though from somewhere or other outside the world. He is here already. Of course we must believe in the transcendence of God. We must think of Him in His eternal being as distinct from the world, "dwelling apart in light unapproachable". Yet, unless He is also immanent in the world, we can know nothing of Him—unless, of course, we suppose that occasionally He steps in from outside, and makes His presence felt by some startling and dramatic act of intervention. But that has become increasingly difficult to believe; and there are perhaps few nowadays except the lawyers who would ascribe unaccountable events to an "act of God". We must hold together the two ideas of God transcendent and God immanent. And belief in the Spirit is belief in the immanence of God—belief that in Him "we live and move and have our being".

Now, the Christian belief in the Spirit was the direct result of the experiences of the first Christians. The New Testament contains two accounts of what they called "the coming of the Spirit"—of what they regarded as the source of their experience of His presence. According to the fourth Gospel the Spirit was the gift of the risen Jesus to His disciples. When He appeared to them on the evening of the first Easter Day, "He *breathed* on them, and saith unto them 'Receive ye the Holy Spirit' "(John xx: 22). According to Acts, the promise of Jesus that they should "receive power", when the Holy Spirit had come upon them, was fulfilled on the day of Pentecost, when the house where they were sitting was filled with the sound of a "mighty wind", and "there appeared unto them tongues parting asunder, like as of fire, and they were all filled with the Holy Spirit" (Acts ii: 2-4). And Peter's explanation of what had happened was that "this Jesus . . . being exalted at the right hand of God, and having received from the Father the promise of the Holy Spirit, hath poured forth this which ye see and hear" (Acts ii: 33). These accounts differ, but both bear witness to an experience of which it was believed that Christ was the author, and which had been made possible by His death and resurrection. That experience is described as the result of the coming of the Spirit.

Now, the Hebrew word of which "spirit" is the translation means properly "wind", or "breath". And the fundamental idea of spirit in the Old Testament is that of active power or energy—a power like that of the strange invisible force which uproots trees, and whirls leaves along the ground. To this wind-like power, was ascribed the appearance of anything abnormal in human conduct. It was the "spirit" that gave Samson his strength, that came mightily upon Saul, that gave certain people unusual skill or wisdom, and that inspired the prophet. So, when we read of the risen Jesus giving the Spirit to His disciples by "breathing" on them, and of the coming of the Spirit at Pentecost as heralded by a sound as of the rushing of a "mighty wind"—we see at once what a close connection there was between the first Christians' idea of the Spirit, and the older idea of wind or breath of God, through which He makes His presence felt in the world. But there were two things in particular which distinguished the Christians' experience of the Spirit from all previous experiences.

(1) It was a *common* experience. In Old Testament times it was the *individual* in whom from time to time the presence of the Spirit was recognised. The first Christians, on the other hand, were conscious of a power which bound them together into a *fellowship*. St. Paul set beside the "grace of Christ" and "love of God" the "fellowship of the Holy Spirit" (2 Corinthians xiii: 14). Of the gifts of the Spirit, the greatest, he said, is love; and in the New Testament, the characteristic Christian virtues are social virtues.

The notion that you can be a Christian by yourself—unattached, as it were—is not a New Testament one. No doubt the Spirit was thought of as dwelling in individuals—but in individuals only as sharing in the common life of the Church.

(2) The second thing that was new in the Christian experience of the Spirit, was its connection with *Jesus*. It had come from Him. In the Old Testament, it is only rarely that the Spirit is thought of as the source of moral goodness. In the New Testament, goodness is the chief sign of His presence. It is true that the old idea lingered on. But for Paul at least, the first fruit of the Spirit was "love, joy, peace, long-suffering, kindness, goodness" (Galatians v: 22). The explanation is clear. It was thus that the Spirit had manifested itself in Jesus. The Spirit was His Spirit—not an impersonal force breathed into men by God, but Jesus Himself set free from the limitations of His earthly life and come to live in His Church. And, therefore, the fruit of the Spirit was to be found, not primarily in those strange and sensational phenomena which some early Christians valued so highly, but in a life conformable to that of Christ. It has often been remarked that Paul's famous chapter on Love (1 Corinthians xiii), that supreme gift of the Spirit, seems to be inspired by the character of Jesus Himself.

So much for the beginnings of the Christian belief in the Spirit. We must go on to consider some of its implications. But here there is one thing to be said. Of all the reasons which led to the ascription of divinity to Christ, none perhaps was more compelling than this experience of the Spirit. If it is true that Christ—as this experience implied—"fills all things" with His presence, it can only be because He has "ascended far above the heavens" (Ephesians iv: 10). Only from the glorified Christ could the Spirit come.

15

I believe in the Holy Ghost

(b)

We have seen that to speak, as the first Christians did, and as many of our hymns and prayers do still, of the "descent" of the Spirit—of the Spirit as *coming down* from heaven, coming upon us, entering into us, is somewhat misleading. It suggests a God who lives somewhere or other outside the world, and occasionally comes into it. But in fact, "God is in the order of nature as a whole, not specifically in what seem to be its gaps". To realise that is important, for the gaps have an inconvenient way of getting filled up. And if God is to be found only in the gaps, there may come a time when there is no room left for Him at all. I think we should do well to substitute, for the distinction between supernatural and natural, that between transcendent and immanent. That is a true distinction. God is, and must be, transcendent— separate from the world, dwelling apart in light unapproachable, and in that sense unknowable. Yet we can know Him in so far as He is immanent in the world. St. Paul said that the more excellent gifts of the Spirit are moral qualities of the Christian life. God speaks to us from within our own consciousness.

c

We cannot really separate the Spirit of God from the spirit of man—as the use of the same word for both itself suggests. Let us look at a few examples of how that works out in practice.

(1) *Prayer.* Most of us know what it is to say our prayers, but seem, as we say them, to be talking either to ourselves, or to the empty air. If we were to stop for a moment and ask ourselves "Why am I praying, at all?" the answer would be reassuring. "Because God is in me." There can be no other answer. "God," said St. Paul, "sent forth the Spirit of His Son into our hearts, crying, Abba, Father" (Galatians iv: 6). He seems to have meant that it is the presence of the Spirit within us, which enables us to speak to God, and call Him Father. We could not do that unless the Spirit of His Son were in us. That is why we *want* to pray. That we want to pray is a proof of God's presence in us. We pray because we are homesick. There is that in us which links us with God. We need not be worried, as we sometimes are, by fear that our apparent awareness of God may be auto-suggestion. If, in fact, it is from within our own consciousness that God speaks to us, the fact that our awareness of Him comes from ourselves is not in itself any proof that it does not come from God. God is in us—or else we should not pray at all; and as St. Augustine said: "Our souls are restless until they rest in Him."

(2) Or, again, consider problems of *conduct*. St. Paul said that "we have the mind of Christ" (1 Corinthians ii: 16). It follows that we can approach problems of conduct with an independence like that of Jesus Himself. It is sometimes supposed that when such problems arise we can solve them by

turning up a text in the Gospels. But a relevant text is not always to be found—and this is not necessary. After all, Jesus was concerned with problems of *His* time, and not of ours. But apart from that it does not seem to have been His intention to provide us with a code of rules. The Spirit, not the letter, was His gift to the world. The only words that He is recorded to have written, He wrote in the dust (John viii: 6). We may perhaps see a parabolic meaning in that. That is not to say—far from it—that we can cut ourselves adrift from the past. The yearly round of Church worship should teach us that. Whit Sunday comes at the *end* of the Church's year. It is only after we have been taken steadily through the events of the life, death, and resurrection of Jesus that we are sent out to face the future in the power of the Spirit which comes as the consequence and climax of all that went before. "We must indeed go back to the Gospels and live again with Jesus in Galilee and at Jerusalem. But we must not *stay* there." St. Paul was always talking of the freedom of the Christian. "Where the Spirit of the Lord is, there is freedom." And he urged the Galatians to "stand fast" in that freedom. (2 Corinthians iii: 17, Galatians v: 1). Such freedom includes the right and duty to think for ourselves. "Why", Jesus asked, "even of your own selves judge ye not what is right?" (Luke xii: 57). Think for yourselves. Find out for yourselves the answer to your problems. And if we seek to learn the mind of Christ, we can be confident that we have *within* us that which "shall guide us into all the truth" (John xvi: 13).

(3) Let us take one last example—*God's commandments.* What does God command? And how are we to find out? Again the answer is that we are to look

within ourselves for God's commands. It is true that the Ten Commandments were said to have been dictated by God to Moses, and inscribed on tables of stone. But, in fact, as St. Paul said in another connection, God's commandments are "written not with ink, but with the Spirit of the living God; not on tables of stone, but on tables that are hearts of flesh" (2 Corinthians iii: 3), i.e. what God commands is that which we ourselves recognise to be right. "A thing is not right", wrote Archbishop Temple, "because God commands it. God commands it because it is right." It is because we see a thing to be right that we recognise it as what God commands. Our insight into what is good may be sadly imperfect. But there is a "light which lights every man"; and in following such light as we can see, we are obeying God's commands. In this, as in everything else, God acts upon us from within ourselves. It is "God's work all of it, and man's work all of it". "I, yet not I". That is not a bad definition of what we mean by belief in the Spirit.

16

I believe in . . . the Holy Catholic Church

This is the belief which follows upon belief in the Holy Spirit. And the fact that the two are so closely connected, is important for our understanding both of the Spirit and of the Church.

(1) We have already noticed that the chief result

of experience of the Spirit was, according to the New Testament, the creation of a fellowship. That, according to St. Paul, was the distinctive gift of the Spirit. The Christianity of the New Testament was essentially a *corporate* religion. To be a Christian was to be a member of the Christian Society: there was no such thing as an isolated or individual saint. To receive the Spirit was "to be drawn out of isolation into the fellowship of the Body of Christ". The Old Testament records God's dealings, not primarily with individuals, but with a *people*. And therefore it is significant that in the New Testament the Church is regarded as the new Israel, the fulfilment of that which had been foreshadowed in the old Israel, a *community* —though not now confined to the people of Israel, but one in which, according to St. Paul, "there is neither Jew nor Greek, circumcision nor uncircumcision, barbarian, Scythian, slave or free" (Galatians iii: 28).

(2) But the connection between the Spirit and the Church is important also for our understanding of the Church. The fact that belief in the Church follows upon belief in the Spirit reminds us that the one is dependent upon the other. There has often been a tendency to exalt the Church to a position higher than that which it is given in the Creed. It is perhaps a mistake to speak of "our mother the Church". The Church is itself the creation of the Spirit. The Spirit comes first—and only then, and subordinate to the Spirit, the Church. It is the Spirit that is the source of our fellowship in the Church. Not only that, but we are surely bound to recognise that the work of the Spirit is not confined to the Church. Wherever we see true fellowship, the drawing

of men together to serve the common good instead of their private interest, there we see the Spirit at work, even though unrecognised.

What, then, we may ask, distinguishes the Church from the world? In what sense is it true that the Church is, peculiarly, the sphere in which the Spirit works? Now, it has been said that "wherever an omnipresent God is specially realised He specially is". And I think we may say that what distinguishes the Church from the world, is not that the Spirit is at work in the one, and not in the other—but that in the Church, the presence of the Spirit is recognised and acknowledged. "The Church is the community in which men *know and confess* what they are, and can become what they are—members of Christ, children of God, and inheritors of the Kingdom of Heaven." All men are children of God—but they do not all know it, and acknowledge it. The Spirit is everywhere present, and everywhere at work. But many are unaware of His presence, even though they may show fruits of it. And the business of the Church is to bear witness to that presence, and exemplify in its own life the fellowship with God, and with one another, which is available for all men. It is clear that it can only bear that witness, and exemplify that fellowship, if it is distinct from the world. The Church is not an end in itself. The prophets of the Old Testament were constantly warning the people of Israel not to imagine that they were God's favourites, and that He was concerned exclusively with their salvation; and the Church is perpetually in need of the same warning. The Church has a mission to the world. It does not exist for itself alone. Yet if it is to carry out its mission, it must be *distinct* from the world.

If it is to be Catholic, it must first be holy. If it is at last to be all-inclusive, it must be separate and distinct. And that means that it must be organised. It must be a recognisable institution, concerned with its own preservation, and, as an institution, be liable to the particular dangers to which all institutions are exposed.

As we know too well, the Church has not escaped these dangers. Its history has been marred by intolerance, undue conservatism, accommodation to the ways of the world, and an absence in itself of that very fellowship of the Spirit which it exists to exemplify and foster. It is no wonder that people have often rebelled against the very idea of institutional Christianity. Such an attitude is natural, but none the less utterly wrong-headed. If the failures of the Church are obvious, no less obvious is the need for its existence and, we may add, its positive achievement. It has at least mediated to us the ideal and standard by which we judge it. It has taught us to recognise its own imperfections. If we can say, as we often do say, that "the Church is not like Christ", that is because it has at least succeeded in handing down to us the Christ-like ideal. Indeed, it has been truly said that "no one would ever have heard of Christianity if there had been no Church". By its ministry of word and sacraments, it has kept the light of the Gospel shining in the world. He who thinks he can get on all right without the Church should think again. However, we must always remember that the *belief* in the Church which the Creed requires depends upon a prior belief in Christ. St. Paul said that "God was in Christ, reconciling the world unto Himself". That is why we are bound to believe that the Church, which that act of God in Christ created, has its place in the purpose of God as a means by which the reconciliation of the world may be effected. However imperfectly, it bears witness to the "dependence of human society on God". And it is difficult to see how that witness could be borne except by a Church, a society which exemplified in its own life that dependence, and sought to bring the whole world into the realisation of it.

17

We have been thinking about the belief in the Church. And it may be well, before we go on to the next clause in the Creed, to say something on a subject which is much in the air at present—the meaning of *Baptism*.

Baptism is a sacrament. The Church of England Catechism defines a sacrament as "an outward and visible sign of an inward and spiritual grace". But what do we mean by "grace"? Grace has often been thought of as a sort of medicine, which God gives us and which we can get through the use of what are called "the means of grace". But we shall be nearer the truth, perhaps, if we think of "means of grace" as "ways of getting into personal relation with God". And there are all kinds of such ways. There is a sense, therefore, in which all our experience of God may be called sacramental. The need for sacraments in the narrower sense comes from the difficulty— if we may put it this way—of finding God anywhere, unless we find Him *somewhere*. The purpose of sacraments in this narrower sense, is two-fold—to express the true relation of our life to God, and so to help us to make that relation actual. They are symbolic, and they are instrumental.

Let us, in the light of all this, consider the sacrament of baptism. And first, in the form in which it appears in the New Testament—that of adult baptism. We can say, shortly, that what it *symbolised* was the truth that God is the Father of men, and they are His children. What it *effected* was the realisation of that truth. It did not make the baptised person the child of God. He was that already. But it helped him to realise it. The effect of baptism on one who had already responded to God's call was, perhaps, largely psychological. "It was a thing most valuable to the Christian in the circumstances of that day, to have a great public experience like this to fall back on, amid doubts and persecutions." "It caused an immense access of certainty, which did not cease to act through life." So we can say, perhaps, that baptism symbolised more than it actually effected. St. Paul could speak of the convert as having risen with Christ in baptism. Yet he found it necessary to urge him to make his life correspond with that ideal. "If ye then be risen with Christ, seek those things that are above, where Christ is" (Colossians iii: 1). Ideally, the convert was already the child of God, and knew that he was—but the full reality of sonship was only potentially his.

However, it was not long before infant baptism became the rule in the Church. It was a natural development; but it raises difficulties, and it opens the way to abuses. For it has not always been realised that there is inevitably a difference between the baptism of children and of adults. The *symbolic* aspect of both is the same. The *instrumental* aspect cannot be the same. The sacrament is an "outward and visible sign of an inward and spiritual grace". Of course, if you think of grace in impersonal terms—as a kind of heavenly something which can be put into us— then there is no difficulty in the idea of a small child receiving, unawares, God's grace. But if grace is a matter of personal influence, then it must depend upon a personal response which a baby cannot give. Is then infant baptism nothing but a symbolic rite? Does it effect nothing at all? Well, the answer must depend on what we believe about the Church. If the Church is the "Body of Christ", if (as it has been said) "God did not manifest Himself in Jesus alone, but in the life of the group which was formed about Him, and in whose creation He was Himself the decisive factor"—then admission to the Church cannot be a matter of no moment for a new-born child. The Spirit—so we believe—is at work primarily in the Church. Not, of course, only there. To suppose that an unbaptised child is excluded from salvation is to set wholly unwarranted limits to the power of God. As we have already seen, what distinguishes the Church from the world is not that the Spirit is at work in the one and not in the other, but that in the Church the presence of the Spirit is recognised and acknowledged. Can we suppose then, that a child gains nothing from the opportunity of growing up from his very earliest days in such an environment? The difference between the effect of baptism on the adult and on the child is put very well by Dr. Forsyth in his book *The Church and the Sacraments*, when he says that "the child is not given the Spirit, but placed where the Spirit moves". *Placed where the Spirit moves.* Why, it is often asked, is baptism apparently so ineffective? Why is there so little difference between the baptised and the unbaptised? The answer surely is that there is no magic about baptism. Whether it is of any effective use will depend upon how far it does, in fact, introduce the child to an environment in which the Spirit moves. "It should be easier to grow up a Christian inside the Church than outside of it." But it will be easier only in so far as the Church, and in particular that small part of the Church in which the child is brought up, is living up to the ideal. And no small part of the value of infant baptism is to be found in its effects on the *parents*, and on the Church as a whole, in the fact that it does, or should, bring home to them their own responsibility to provide for the child an environment in which it is really true that "the Spirit moves", and in which there is some hope that he may be able to grow to "the measure of the stature of the fulness of Christ".

18

I believe in . . . the Communion of Saints

This clause was a late addition to the Creed, and there is no evidence of its use till near the end of the fourth century. Moreover, there seems to be some doubt as to why it was put in, and what it was intended to mean. Many different interpretations have been suggested: we are at liberty to choose the one which we prefer. For myself, the interpretation which I like best, and which, I think, is a legitimate one, is that which takes it to express what has been called "the intimate union and conjunction of all believers with one another in Christ—a union not broken by death". That the Church is an organism which derives its unity from Christ, is part, at least, of what St. Paul meant when he spoke of the Church as the Body of Christ. "We," he said, "who are many, are one body in Christ" (Romans xii: 5). And since he could speak of the "dead in Christ", and believe that when he died he would be "with Christ" (1 Thessalonians iv: 16, Philippians i: 23), it would seem to follow that the unity of the Body of Christ is one which cannot be broken by death. If both the living and the dead are "in Christ", then their communion with one another is not broken.

Now, if the Communion of Saints means the "fellowship of all believers with one another in Christ", we must give to the word "saints" a meaning which it commonly has in the New Testament—a meaning different from that which we normally give to it. By "saints" we commonly mean, in the words of the Epistle to the Hebrews, "spirits of just men made perfect" (Hebrews xii: 23). In the New Testament, and notably in St. Paul's Epistles, the saints are *all* the members of the Church without distinction. The meaning of the Latin word from which "saint" is derived, and of the corresponding Greek word, is "holy". It is the same word as is used of the "Holy Spirit" and "Holy Church". And in all three cases it means the same thing: "that which belongs to

God, or is set apart for His service". It is in this sense that members of the Church are holy. They are holy because of their divine calling. It is their duty, of course, to try and make themselves worthy of this high calling. But it does not follow that they are yet worthy. So we find in the First Epistle of Peter (i: 15) the exhortation: "Like as he who called you is holy, be ye yourselves holy in all manner of living; because it is written: Ye shall be holy, for I am holy." It has sometimes been maintained that the Church should consist only of those who are holy in this sense—that membership of the Church should be confined to those who reach a certain standard of goodness, and that unworthy members should be excluded. But such an idea has always been rejected by the Church as a whole—and for at least two very good reasons: (1) Because the line between worthy and unworthy is a very difficult one to draw. To identify the more obvious and open forms of evil is easy. But Jesus said that what God requires is inward purity. And therefore we shall be wise not to pose as judges, but leave judgment to Him who alone "can discern the thoughts and intents of the heart". In the parable of the Tares, Jesus showed that it was no less foolish to try and separate the good from the bad, than it would be to try and remove weeds from a field of wheat. You will almost certainly pull up the wheat along with the weeds. So it is best to "let both grow together till the harvest" (Matthew xiii: 24ff.). (2) And the second reason can be put quite shortly. It would surely be wrong to exclude from the sphere in which the Holy Spirit works those who most need His help. Excommunication is a desperate remedy. Members of the Church then may be "saints" in the making; they are not necessarily saints in fact; and the idea of a "pure Church" in this world is certainly not a New Testament one.

Belief in the Communion of Saints is, therefore, according to our definition, belief in the fellowship of *all* believers in Christ. And further, it is a fellowship that is not broken by death—and that because it is a fellowship in Him who has overcome death. In the words of Charles Wesley's hymn:

> One family we dwell in Him,
>   One Church above, beneath,
> Though now divided by the stream,
>   The narrow stream of death.

The desire to find a bridge over the stream of death, by which the living may communicate with the departed, is a natural one. And the popularity of Spiritualism, which claims to provide such a bridge, is not surprising. The Christian, too, believes in the existence of such a bridge, but a wholly different one from that which Spiritualism offers. The Spiritualist believes that he can communicate with the departed through a human medium. The Christian believes that his fellowship with the departed is mediated through Christ. If communion of the Christian with Christ is not broken by death, then neither can his communion with his fellow Christians be broken.

The recorded teaching of Jesus contains hardly any reference to the conditions of life in the next world. And the reason is clear. It is with *this* life that we are concerned, and morbid curiosity about the next life would distract our attention from what should be our immediate and pressing concern. We find eternal life, not by peering through the gate of death, but by ascending in heart and mind to the things that are above. The writer of the fourth Gospel defined eternal life as knowledge of God, and of Him whom He sent, even Jesus Christ. The fuller our knowledge of Christ, and the closer our fellowship with Him, the more real may be our sense of fellowship with all who are in Christ, on whatever side of the stream of death they may be. In Christ we are all one; and death cannot destroy that unity. If so, we must surely believe that to *pray* for the departed is not only legitimate but inevitable. We should not be prejudiced against the idea of praying for the departed because of its association with the use of prayers and ceremonies to relieve the suffering of souls in Purgatory. There is no necessary connection. If our communion with those whom we love is not broken by death, how can we cease to pray for them as we did when alive? Indeed, it is precisely in prayer that we may expect to realise most keenly our fellowship with them, and may know that we are "knit together in one communion and fellowship, in the mystical Body of Christ our Lord".

19

I believe in . . . the Forgiveness of sins

(a)

In the Creed, confession of belief in the Church and the Communion of Saints is followed by that of

belief in the forgiveness of sins. That is a comforting
thought. As members of the Church we are "called
to be saints". And vain indeed would be that calling,
were there not coupled with it the promise of
forgiveness. Now, to understand what is meant by
the forgiveness of sins, we must first be clear as to the
meaning of sin. Sin is a word which is often loosely
used of any wrong act. But, in fact, you cannot
properly use the word outside the sphere of religion.
A crime, for example, is a transgression of a law of the
State: it is not necessarily a sin. A sin is an offence
against God. The idea of sin, therefore, depends
upon belief in God. "In a godless world there would
be no such thing as sin." And further, we must be
careful not to confuse "sins" with "sin". By *sin* is
meant a state of alienation from God, which leads
to *sins*. It is significant, therefore, that the teaching
of Jesus was teaching about God, rather than about
sin. For it is only awareness of God, and so of our
alienation from Him, that can make us aware of our
sinfulness, and so of our need for forgiveness.

Now, forgiveness of sins has always been closely
connected with the death of Christ on the Cross. But
we shall be better able to understand this connection,
if we consider first what is the real nature of our need.
You will often hear people say that our chief religious
need is for the removal from our hearts of the burden
of guilt. I don't know about others—but for myself I
am quite sure that my chief need is, not to have the
burden removed, but to be made to feel the weight
of it. It is the saints, those who carry the lightest
burden, who are most conscious of its weight. "Christ
Jesus came into the world to save sinners; of whom
I am chief" (1 Timothy i: 15). I don't know whether

St. Paul himself said that, but it is something which only a St. Paul could honestly say. Most of us, if we said it, would know that it was humbug. We don't think of ourselves as the chief of sinners. We don't feel the weight of our burden—and until we do, we are not likely to want it removed. No doubt it is true that our chief need is for forgiveness. But there is something which must come before forgiveness, and that is repentance. And the trouble about sin is precisely that the more you sin, the less aware of it you become, and the less inclined, therefore, to repent. It has been truly said, that "the natural consequence of the commission of wrong, is not the awakening but the dulling of the sense of sin". It would almost be true to say, that the better you feel, the worse you are. The Pharisee in the parable was not by any means a thoroughly bad man, but what was wrong with him was that he thought he was all right; whereas what was right with the Publican was that he knew he was all wrong. And so it was he who "went down to his house justified rather than the other". We can see, therefore, what a complete misreading of the teaching of Jesus it is to suppose (as has often been popularly supposed) that He preached a gospel of easygoing tolerance. "God won't be too hard on you." Forgiveness of that kind could only aggravate the disease from which we need to be cured. It is not an anaesthetic that we need—we are far too insensitive as it is—but something that will prick us into sensitivity. The first step towards a cure is to be made to feel the pain of our sickness. And in this sense punishment is a very necessary stage on the road to forgiveness. But the punishment that is necessary is not the arbitrary infliction of pain or suffering, but that which comes from the discovery of the inherent evil of the sin itself. It is the hurt of the sin itself, not of some consequence of it, that we need to feel. And here is the problem. For the more we sin, the more immune are we from the pain of it. That we should somehow be made conscious of the evil of our sin is, then, the first need that any doctrine of the Atonement must meet.

But let us suppose that by some means or other our sense of sin is awakened. What then? Can the effects of our sin be undone? Well, in one sense, of course, they cannot. It is impossible to alter the past in the sense of actually undoing what has been done. It has been done, and nothing can alter the fact. Our repentance cannot of itself repair the mischief we have done to others. A murderer cannot bring his victim back to life. Here, then, is another problem to which any doctrine of Redemption must provide an answer. But there is another sense in which the effects of sin *can* be undone. For it is true enough that "the essence of sin lies not in the thing done, but in the will of him who did it". And, therefore, when once our will has been changed, our sin has become as though it had never been. Righteousness, as St. Paul saw clearly, is not a matter of good deeds done, but of our present attitude of mind. Conversion of our will carries with it abolition of our sin. And we need not brood upon our past failures, and imagine that our character has been marked with an indelible stain. For our repentance has removed the stain: we can put the past behind us, and make a new start. The Publican in the parable went down to his house justified. But we come back again to the crucial question: How are we to be induced to repent? That is the problem of Redemption. To the solution that Christianity offers we must now turn.

20

I believe in . . . the Forgiveness of Sins

(b)

The Christian belief in the forgiveness of sins is based partly on the teaching of Jesus, partly on the universal experience of Christians that, as St. Paul said, "in Christ we have our redemption" (Ephesians i: 7). That God's property is "to have mercy and to forgive" is a recurring refrain of the teaching of Jesus. He justified His assurance by such parables as those of the Prodigal Son and the Lost Sheep; and in the end He paid for it by His death. He died because He refused to deny His belief in the unchanging love of God—a love which is conditioned by nothing whatever but the sinner's willingness to accept it. But it is precisely that condition which it is so difficult to fulfil. The effect of sin is to destroy the sense of sin. The more you sin the less it hurts you, and the less, therefore, you want to be rid of it. How are we to be made to feel its pain, and so to seek release from it? That is the problem. And it is a problem which many of the older theories of Atonement seem hardly to have recognised. Their object was to explain how it might be made possible for God to forgive: the devil, it was said, must be paid his price—man's debt to God must be made good—God's justice must be satisfied. Those who put forward these theories were "all engaged in explaining how God overcame a difficulty". But the real problem is how *we* are to overcome a difficulty—how it is to be made possible not for God to forgive—but for us to repent. It is God's nature and property to forgive; but we don't want His forgiveness.

The problem of forgiveness is the problem of repentance. How are we to be made to feel the pain of the sin, which, the more we sin, hurts less and less? Well—the answer was foreshadowed in Isaiah's picture of the Servant of God. He told how, seeing the suffering of the Servant, people were moved to exclaim: "Surely he hath borne our griefs and carried our sorrows. He was wounded for our transgressions—he was bruised for our iniquities—with his stripes we are healed" (Isaiah liii: 4, 5). There is a way—and it is the only way—by which you can be brought to feel the hurt of the sin which you have become too insensitive to feel yourself, and that is be seeing how much it hurts somebody else. Someone must suffer for your sin—someone good enough to feel what you are not good enough to feel. That is the way of Redemption—and it is continually exemplified in every day life. The work of Redemption goes on because there are, here and there, people good enough to feel the hurt of sin, to bear the stripes which bring healing to the rest of us. Of this the death of Christ on the Cross is the final and pre-eminent demonstration. There we see "focussed in one vivid moment" what sin means and how it may be cured. The death of Jesus happened long ago. But it is a symbol of what is always happening—"the bursting forth through historical conditions of the very nature of the

Everlasting". We see there that in the heart of God there is a distress far deeper than any we have ever known ourselves, and that we are ourselves the cause of that distress.

> It was my pride and hardness
> That hung Him on the Tree:
> Those cruel nails, O Saviour,
> Were driven in by me.

"We see our own secret selves [so it has been said] staring out at us in the face of the rigorous and self-righteous Pharisee or of the lax and worldly Sadducee, in the treachery of Judas betraying the best he knew, or in the denial of Peter forsaking that to which he owed everything." "We all find ourselves at some time or other assistants at the Passion." And to find ourselves there, is the beginning of our cure. It means that the natural effect of sin in hardening the heart and destroying the sense of sin has begun to be reversed. Our conscience has been awakened, and we are ready to accept the forgiveness which God offers to everyone who wants it. The problem of repentance has been solved: "with His stripes we are healed".

To that many of our hymns on the Passion give clear expression. But they are apt to lay too exclusive stress on what Christ has done for the *individual*. Salvation has often been thought of as the rescue of individuals from a world that is doomed to destruction.

But we are part of that world. We are *not* mere individuals; and we cannot be content with the saving of our own souls. To talk of "saving your own soul" suggests that you might get to heaven all by yourself. But salvation of the individual must depend on salvation of the society of which the individual is a part. We need what has been called a "cosmic" Saviour. St. Paul recognised this. He was aware that the sin of an individual was the result of what he called *Sin*—with a capital S. He did not believe in the total depravity of the human race; but he did believe that Sin was not merely an individual, but a corporate thing. And surely he was right. Of no single individual can it be said that he is solely responsible for the wrong that he does. There are degrees of guilt of course. But in the end our individual sins are the result of a corporate wrongness; and for this, and not merely for the sin of individuals, any doctrine of the Atonement must provide a remedy. St. Paul, at least, believed that the Cross of Christ does provide such a remedy: "God was in Christ, reconciling the *world* to Himself." The Incarnation is the pledge that God does not stand outside the world, but that He is *in* it. The Creator is Himself the Redeemer. Indeed, there is a sense in which Creation and Redemption are the same thing. The healing power of God is in the world, bringing good out of evil, undoing the mischief that is caused by sin, mischief of which our own sin is in part the cause, and which of ourselves we can do so little to undo. And the purpose of our own forgiveness is not merely our own personal salvation. It is a call to take our share in God's work, and become "not just the passive recipients, but the active agents of His redeeming action".

21

I believe in . . . the Resurrection of the body

An early Christian author said of Jesus that He had
"abolished death, and brought life and immortality
to light". And a modern writer has said that "while
it would not indeed be true to say that nothing at all
would be left of the Christian system if eternal life
were denied—yet what would be left would certainly
not be Christianity. From the beginning the Faith
has been one with the Hope." That is worth remem-
bering at a time like the present, when belief in a
future life tends to be regarded as at best one of the
less important articles of the Christian faith. Now, the
most characteristic feature of the Christian belief
about the life to come, is this belief in the resurrection
of the body. And we must consider what is meant
by it.

The phrase "resurrection of the *body*" is an English
modification of the original wording of the Creed,
which was "resurrection of the flesh" (one fourth-
century Creed actually said "of *this* flesh"). And in
the Baptism Service in the Prayer Book of 1662, the
words still appear in the form "resurrection of the
flesh". It is probably true to say that until quite
recent times, the majority of Christian people believed that "on the resurrection morning soul and
body meet again". The influence of that belief can be
seen in our funeral customs, in the almost super-

stitious reverence that is felt for the place of burial, and in the still common dislike of cremation. That at the resurrection there will be a reunion of the soul with the actual physical body which has been laid in the grave, is, incredible as it may seem, a view which has commonly been held. But, in refusing to accept it, we can appeal not only to common sense, but to the authority of the New Testament. St. Paul, though he believed that in the next life we should not be disembodied spirits, yet was quite clear that "flesh and blood cannot inherit the Kingdom of God" (1 Corinthians xv: 50). And we can be pretty sure that it was not the belief of Jesus either. On the only occasion when He is recorded to have spoken about the resurrection (when challenged by the Sadducees to admit the absurdity of a belief which involved the possibility that a woman might find herself confronted in the next life by seven husbands), He replied: "When they shall rise from the dead, they neither marry nor are given in marriage, but are as angels in heaven" (Mark xii: 25). The body that would be raised, He clearly meant, would not be the actual body of flesh and blood that had been laid in the grave. The idea that it would be is perhaps partly due to mistaken ideas about the nature of the risen body of Christ. But there can be few enlightened Christians at the present day, who believe in the resurrection of the physical body.

What, then, do we mean when we say that we believe in the resurrection of the body? When you say that you believe in "life after death", you may mean one of two things. (1) You may mean that the soul is of such a nature that it survives the death of the body. That is not necessarily a religious belief

at all. The evidence for it may be scientifically in-
vestigated: the Society for Psychical Research under-
takes to do so, and claims to have found purely
scientific grounds for believing it. Or (2) you may
mean, not that the soul is by nature immortal, but
that it has the capacity, by communion with God, to
rise to a higher kind of life—a life which is not a
natural property of the soul but a gift of God. That
is a purely religious belief, and cannot be proved
scientifically. It depends upon belief in God, and
cannot exist apart from such belief. Such is the Christian idea of life after death. It is belief not in survival
of death—but in resurrection from death to life. It
takes death seriously and recognises its reality. It
does not try to pretend, like the Spiritualists, that
there is really no such thing, and that you simply,
(as they say) "pass over" into another realm of
existence. It recognises also that eternal life is not
something which is ours by nature, but something
which God offers us on condition that we are willing
to pay the price of winning it. The price is surrender
of *this* life. So Jesus taught. "Whosoever would save
his life, shall lose it; and whosoever shall lose his life,
shall save it." Death is the gateway to life. Christianity
is the religion of the Cross. Lose all to gain all. Die to
live. To the disciples who asked for a good place in
the Kingdom of God, Jesus replied with the search-
ing question, "Are ye able to drink the cup that I
drink?" (Mark x: 38). Eternal life is not simply a
prolongation of this life—which is, after all, not an
attractive prospect. It is life of a higher quality than
the life of earth—a life which can only be obtained
through death and resurrection—and which, though
we can and must begin to enter upon it now, can

only be consummated in eternity. But to that we
must turn when we go on to consider belief "in the
life everlasting".

22

I believe in . . . the life everlasting

"I come that they may have life, and may have it
more abundantly" (John x: 10). So said the Christ
of the fourth Gospel. And as the climax of the Creed,
we express our faith in the truth of that declaration—
in the reality of that life, full and abundant, which
Christ came into the world to give us. Our task, in
this last chapter, is to consider the nature of this life
which Christ offers us. It is described here as "life
everlasting"; and that seems to imply that its chief
characteristic is that it goes on for ever. Someone once
told me that he sincerely hoped there was no truth
in the idea of a future life. The thought of it filled him
with horror—and no wonder. For he imagined the
future life as an unending continuation of *this* life—
and he had had enough of that already. But the Greek
word of which "everlasting" is a translation really
means "pertaining to an age". As used in the New
Testament, it means "pertaining to a particular age
—the age to come". As applied to "life" then, it
means the kind of life that is characteristic of the
age to come—"the life of the world to come", as
the Nicene Creed has it.

What can we know of that life? St. Paul said that

the "light of the knowledge of the glory of God shone in the face of Jesus Christ" (2 Corinthians iv: 6). Christ then can tell us, if anyone can, what the life of heaven is like. The life that He lived here on earth is the fullest revelation that we have of the life of the world to come. In trying, accordingly, to imagine the life of heaven, we shall not go far wrong if we think of it as at least not different in kind from the highest life we know on earth. Of course, since eternal life is life in God, it is life which cannot be destroyed. But it is by its quality, rather than duration, that it is differentiated from ordinary life. And, therefore, it is a life that we can begin to live now. That was the teaching of the fourth Gospel. "He that heareth my word, and believeth Him that sent me, hath eternal life, and cometh not into judgment, but hath passed out of death into life" (John v: 24). And this life is said to consist in "the knowledge of God and of His Son Jesus Christ" (John xvii: 3). It follows, therefore, that psychical research or the spiritualistic séance can give us no assurance of immortality in the Christian sense. We shall not learn anything about eternal life by looking through the key-hole of the gate of death. Indeed, it is clearly God's purpose that an impenetrable veil should separate this present life from whatever lies beyond —and that, because eternal life, if it is to be found at all, must be found now. We find it, not by dying in a physical sense, but by being spiritually re-born. And now is our chance, and so far as we know, our only chance, to undergo that spiritual re-birth. Now, if ever, we must "ascend in heart and mind to the things that are above". But those who do so ascend, catch hold, as it were, of something which death cannot end. It is commonly supposed that we are each of us endowed with a soul at birth. I often wonder whether it would not be truer to think of ourselves as endowed with the capacity for *creating* a soul. Keats called this world "the vale of soul-making". That, he said, is the use of the world—"to school an intelligence and make it a soul".

Now there are few of us who have not had at least some small experience of what Christianity calls eternal life. Francis Thompson saw

. . . the traffic of Jacob's ladder
Pitched between Heaven and Charing Cross.

But it would be a fatal mistake to suppose that it is only to the mystic that is given this vision of "something beyond". "The modern man," so B. H. Streeter said in an essay on *The life of the world to come*, "who is not habituated to expressing the ideals which most appeal to him in religious phraseology, will be disposed to define the highest life as consisting in absolute devotion to the triad: Goodness, Beauty and Truth. Is this," he asks, "essentially different from St. John's definition—the knowledge of God, and of His Son Jesus Christ?" It is true, of course, that such devotion to the highest we know may not have any conscious connection with God and Christ; and without that connection it cannot properly be described as devotion to God. Yet, on the other hand, as Streeter points out, "it is not possible really to know and serve God unless we recognise Him, not only as the Personal Reality over and above the totality of things, but also as actually present and directly manifested through nature and through men in the actual world given to us by sense and

thought". That is the principle of the Incarnation—
that God is revealed in His world. You don't find
Him by leaving this world, and seeking for Him
somewhere outside. Here He is to be found, if we
are to find Him at all. We must follow the light that
we see—for it is the light of God. There are all kinds
of ways in which we are made aware of it; but all
can be summed up under the three headings of
Goodness—Truth—and Beauty. We see it, for
instance, in those ideals of goodness which our in-
most heart tells us we should be ready to die for
rather than betray; above all, in that crowning
ideal of *love*—of which St. John was constrained to
say that "we know that we have passed out of death
into life, because we love the brethren" (1 John iii:
14). We see it again in the attractive power of truth—
which leads scientist or philosopher to devote his
life to its discovery. That there should be any sort
of opposition between the quest of truth and
religion—that the scientist should look with suspicion
upon the religious person, and the religious person
be afraid that if he thinks too much, he will lose his
faith, is the result of an all too narrow idea of God.
The call of truth is the call of God, and desire for
truth is desire for God. And the beauty of the world,
no less, declares to us the glory of God. The religious
person has often been a little contemptuous of the
appeal of beauty, and has made his places of worship
drab and bare—because he feared that beauty
would distract him from the contemplation of
God.

Yet that Jesus did not share his fear, is clear from His
saying about the lilies of the field, and the conviction,
which governed all His teaching, that the world is

God's world, and therefore, that "the whole earth is full of His glory".

Goodness, Truth, and Beauty—surely they all bring us some knowledge of the God who reveals Himself through them, and therefore some understanding and experience of that eternal life which is "knowledge of God". No doubt it is true that "eye hath not seen, nor ear heard, neither have entered into the heart of man, the things that God hath prepared for them that love Him" (1 Corinthians ii: 9). Yet partial and imperfect as our present experience of it may be, it is the basis of our hope for a fuller and more complete realisation of it. That hope, therefore, is not mere wishful thinking. "We seek after the city which is to come", because we have *seen* it, if only from far off; because we have had, at least, some vision of God, and have heard some fragments of the music that is played in heaven— because we have at least begun to live a life which death cannot end.